transparent

transparent

elspeth pridham

MITCHELL BEAZLEY

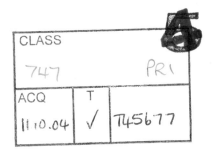
First published in 2003 by Mitchell Beazley,
an imprint of Octopus Publishing Group Ltd,
2–4 Heron Quays, London
E14 4JP

ISBN 1 84000 604 8

A CIP catalogue copy of this book is available
from the British Library

Commissioning Editor **Emma Clegg**
Executive Art Editor **Auberon Hedgecoe**
Senior Editors **Lara Maiklem, Emily Anderson**
Picture Researcher **Jo Walton**
Designer **Emily Wilkinson**
Production Controller **Kieran Connelly**
Copy Editor **Lindsay Porter**
Proofreader **Barbara Mellor**
Indexer **Helen Snaith**

Set in InterFace DaMa and News Gothic

Printed and bound in China by
Toppan Printing Company Limited

contents

introduction

"When the material defining space has transparent qualities, the mode of spatial definition changes categorically." George Papadopoulos, Yorgos Architectural Glass The materials used both for the structures and the objects in our interior spaces define the space as much as the designs to which they are applied. When transparent or translucent materials are used in the spaces that we inhabit, these objects take on a particularly personal relationship with the interior — simply because you can see through and beyond them.

left Back-lit translucent plastic panels add interest to this reception area.
The desk, which is the first point of contact, becomes the focal point.

Let there be light

Not only do windows provide us with visual access to the world outside, they also let the daylight flood in. Given the choice, office workers will always position their desks next to a window. The most popular tables in restaurants are those with a view of the street, and kitchens are invariably designed with the sink under the window so that the chore of washing up can be enhanced by a view of the garden.

Human beings need exposure to natural light. Electricity has enabled us to create artificial light throughout our domestic and commercial environments and yet, although practical, this artificial light is no substitute for natural light. Whether we are at home or at work, research has established that we perform much better with access to natural light. Bright sunlight is particularly mood enhancing, but even the gentle light on a cloudy day can lift our spirits. Plenty of natural light, combined with the feeling that we are not totally enclosed, is conducive to good mental and physical health. Natural light also has the advantage of changing throughout the day, and each time of day brings a different mood and ambience to a room. From the pale tones of dawn, through the bright sunlight of midday, to the soft glow of evening, the changing light affects not only the appearance of our surroundings, but also our patterns of behaviour.

The desire to maximize the flow of light in our enclosed environments has led to an increasing use of glass in architecture for walls, floors, and roofs — not just for commercial buildings, but also for contemporary housing. There is also a strong market for glass conservatories and sunrooms in period properties. Efficient insulation, double glazing, and central heating have allowed us to live and work comfortably within glass structures, so even if it is wet and cold outside, the inside of the house remains warm and welcoming.

right This clear glass screen affords maximum visibility while making the small bathroom seem much larger. The screen is gently curved to echo the shape of the shower tray and to prevent water from splashing on to the floor.

left The use of plastic in the transparent portfolio has led to an increased use of colour. Kartell's yellow La Marie chair is made from a sheet of transparent polycarbonate, and makes an eye-catching feature in the corner of the room.

The increased use of glass has been accompanied by advances in glass technology that have made possible the production of much larger expanses of glass. Using small panes of glass within windows is hardly a new idea, but it was not until 1959, when float glass was invented by Alastair Pilkington, that the mass production of high-quality flat glass began. It was with the subsequent development of laminating (the bonding of two or more sheets of glass using a resin interlayer) that it became possible to use large sheets of glass as load-bearing components in architectural design. Glass can now be used not only for windows, but also to replace bricks or concrete in the construction of walls, floors, ceilings, and staircases. Strong glass panels can even be set into the floor or exterior pavement at ground level, so allowing valuable natural light to reach dark basement rooms that had hitherto been reliant on artificial light.

Despite the increased use of glass in the exterior shell of contemporary buildings, there is still a requirement to ensure the effective internal circulation of natural light. Many projects, particularly office blocks, are now built on such a large scale that they have significant internal space where whole areas are deprived of natural light. The answer is to incorporate transparent materials throughout the building, so that offices, meeting rooms, and other areas are partitioned off with glass walls or screens. The same principle can be applied to domestic dwellings, where internal, windowless rooms can still benefit from natural light if the existing solid walls are replaced with transparent sections.

Loft-style apartments and open-plan homes are now internationally popular dwellings. From London to Tokyo the gradual move is away from the traditional home, where areas were compartmentalized into living room, kitchen, bathroom, and bedroom, to the creation of larger multifunctional spaces with fewer dividing walls. This allows for a far more relaxed style of living, conducive to better communication and shared experiences, with several activities taking place in the same room at the same time — a style of home that embraces transparent materials.

Transparency versus privacy

Although a building constructed entirely with transparent materials may be an appealing idea, the one obvious drawback is the issue of privacy. Although we benefit from exposure to natural light, humans also need private spaces. This applies equally within our domestic interiors and in the office, where meetings and discussions need to be kept confidential. The need for privacy, however, does not require blocking out the light. Translucent materials will still allow light to filter through a barrier while also concealing the identity and activity of those beyond. Translucent materials create psychological barriers in the office, bathroom, or changing room, allowing us to enjoy a sense of privacy and security without being totally detached from the surrounding activity.

There are several methods of transforming glass from transparent to translucent: these range from sandblasting and etching, to incorporating sheets of opaque laminates. Structural elements such as glass walls, floors, and stair treads can be treated across their surface, or designs can be developed to incorporate areas of both transparency and translucency. Creating designs within glass can also be a useful device for developing corporate identities, by featuring a company name or logo within the fabric of the building.

Glass alternatives

Glass has a long history, and was highly prized by ancient cultures from the Egyptians to the Romans. Because it can be applied to designs from windows to wine glasses, it is the material most readily associated with transparent design. There is, however, a wealth of other transparent and translucent materials, each with its own particular properties and features. As glass can be produced in large spans and laminated to produce load-bearing strength, it is the most suitable material for use in construction. Transparent plastic sheets do not have the same degree of

right Even solid materials can let light through when they are worked into a grid or mesh. The cane for this armchair has been woven into a very open structure so that the chair loses some of its substance and no longer dominates the room.

strength, but they can be used effectively for internal walls and screens. Acrylic and polycarbonate, for example, are both transparent plastics that have been used to create imaginative interior walls in locations where the undisturbed passage of light is a design requirement. Other plastics, such as soft, pliant PVC and opaque polypropylene, have been used for contemporary furniture.

Celluloid, the first plastic, was invented in 1870. But plastic as a material for interior furniture and furnishings did not become popular until the 1960s. The use of plastic has been increasing steadily ever since, gradually shedding its original image as a cheap, mass-produced product as designers find new and innovative ways to use this versatile material. Clear plastic is enjoying greater exposure in the production of everyday items, from clear acrylic cutlery to the see-through polycarbonate casing of the iMac.

The transparent interior

In interiors with transparent elements, there is no place for dark furniture and solid fittings; light, bright spaces demand furnishings that follow the same aesthetic. The range of transparent materials presented here identifies international designers who have created pieces for every room in the house using transparent and translucent materials. Some of these designs are functional, such as the Perspex lights by British designer Jona Hoad, others purely decorative, such as the fluorescent Lucciola gauze by the Swiss company Création Baumann. But one element that all these designs have in common is that they work with light – both natural and artificial.

For the living room, there are clear glass tables and coloured PVC chairs; in the bathroom, glass has been used to create stunning baths and basins, while transparent plastics make their own contribution in the form of shower curtains, acrylic toilet seats, and even resin soap dishes and tiles. Translucent cabinet doors in the kitchen and bedroom create a greater sense of space while allowing the contents of the cupboard to make a colourful contribution to the

left Densely woven fabric still allows a degree of natural or artificial light to filter through. A rainbow effect can be achieved by selecting lengths of cloth in a co-ordinating colour palette.

décor of the room. From light fittings to wardrobes and door handles to armchairs, there are transparent products available to complete the detail of any see-through interior.

As well as glass and plastics, designs have been created in materials such as metal and wood, whose substance does not have any transparent qualities. These materials can, however, be adapted and manipulated so that they join the transparent portfolio. Metal grids can be extremely useful as screens, balustrades, or stair treads in the open-plan environment, allowing light to pass through as well as providing visual access to what lies beyond. Wire mesh has also been used effectively in furniture design, from the famous 1951 Diamond chair by Italian designer Harry Bertoia to the contemporary pieces made under the Meshman label by British designer James Gott. Fine wire can even be woven to make highly durable, fire-resistant sheer fabrics, and sheet metal has been used to create innovative modern screens, such as those produced by the British company Full Blown Metals out of a series of inflated steel pillows. Wood is another solid material particularly suited to screens, from the ornate latticework three-fold screens of the Middle East, to flat contemporary screens constructed out of fine sheets of translucent wood veneer. Portable screens are also enjoying a renewed level of interest, as we endeavour to make our living and workspaces multi-functional and adaptable. Lengths of wood can also be used to make openwork seating, and with the recent technological advances in heat-treating timber such pieces of furniture need not have rigid square lines, but can be bent into soft, undulating curves. Other translucent materials, such as sheer fabrics, eggshell fine porcelain, and Japanese paper, can be incorporated into the transparent interior as window treatments, light fittings, and elegant shoji screens.

Clear and frosted glass, plain and patterned plastics, sheer translucent fabrics, and grid structures provide us with an extensive vocabulary of see-through materials from which to create modern interiors that are open-plan, airy, and suffused with natural light.

right Sheets of perforated steel have been used to clad this stairway, creating a smart, slick result while providing the strength and security necessary for stairs. The use of openwork steel allows the sculptural effect of the stair treads to show through.

"I like to pay special attention to the spaces created between solid shapes: often it's the shape of the spaces that makes the design." Tom Schneider, furniture designer The use of clear glass has come to symbolize the core character of the contemporary interior – harnessed both in furniture and in architectural design, its transparency, combined with its material solidity, seems to embody the very essence of a modern space.

left A sense of drama was created in this apartment by using clear glass as the main material for the upstairs floor.

left The most obvious attraction of using large areas of clear glass is to maximize the view. A panorama of London provides the ever-changing backdrop to this boardroom, while the glass desk does nothing to dilute the effect.

right A clear glass door prevents a shower cubicle from becoming a dark and unappealing corner of the bathroom. Here the idea has been taken a stage further with the addition of a glass side panel, while the clear glass shelves provide useful storage.

There is something intrinsically appealing about clear glass. Whether used structurally for walls, floors, or ceilings or on a smaller scale for chairs, baths, or tables, glass has a potent appeal. The crystal clear nature of the material attracts us and allows us total visual access to what lies beyond. And we are fascinated by its uses, finding it hard to accept that something so transparent, so lacking in substance, can also be so strong.

Glass is made by heating a mixture of dissolved silica (which occurs in the form of quartz, sand, or flint) and silicates (which are in any salt or silicic acid) with calcium carbonate (soda) and calcium oxide (lime). Early glass panes were created by blowing molten glass onto metal cooling sheets. The resulting glass carried many faults and air bubbles and could only be used as very small panes set into a supporting frame, as in leaded or mullioned windows. Cast plate glass originated in France in the eighteenth century and was the main method for glass production until 1959, when Englishman Alastair Pilkington created float glass, a cheaper method of mass production that was to become the universal process for the manufacture of high-quality flat glass. Then, with the development of laminate glass, the process by which two or more sheets of glass are bonded together using a resin interlayer to give it strength, it finally became possible to use glass as a construction material.

Over the last ten years there has been considerable interest in the creative use of glass both structurally and for furniture. Designers and manufacturers have been pushing the boundaries to see just how strong and how flexible glass can be. With improved production processes and advances in technology such as laminating and heat treating, it is now possible to produce large sheets of faultless, clear glass strong enough for use as walls, floors, and stairways. The development of UV bonding and precision-cutting tools has resulted in functional everyday pieces, such as chairs and baths, being created out of sheet glass.

The profile of glass within design may wax and wane in future decades, but now it has entered the design portfolio with such confidence it will always provide a viable alternative to more conventional materials.

Bathrooms are well suited to the use of see-through elements, because water and glass — both transparent, after all — complement each other so well. Clear glass has long been used for shower cubicles, because this opens up an otherwise enclosed area to the rest of the bathroom and gives the user a much greater sense of space. But now glass is also being used for baths and basins as an alternative to the more traditional ceramic options. A glass basin or bath, once full, is an extremely inviting prospect, especially if light is designed to shine through the water from below. The water can be viewed not just from above but from the sides, appearing in suspension and unrestricted by its container. Add to this the natural green tint apparent on the edges of glass sheets and the aquatic impact of the glass bathroom is complete.

Glass gives a sharp, clean look and it suits a minimalist style. Glass fittings can also make a small room seem much bigger, because they let light through and give the impression of taking up very little space. Advances in glass bonding have spawned a whole new generation of sanitary glass products. As well as moulded, round basins that can be either free-standing on the counter or an integral part of a glass vanity top, there is now the option of square or oblong fittings made by bonding side sections onto a flat base. Specialist glass company The Igloo has taken this process a stage further by creating a bath made entirely from glass. Two clear sheets of 15-mm (3/4-in) toughened glass are bonded to the 25-mm (1-in) laminated base and end panels with silicon extrusion gaskets, and clamped in place by seven metal rods. The bath is fitted with a chrome overflow and plug and just needs wall-mounted taps to make it fully functional. The beauty of this 1,860-mm (6-ft) bath lies in the simplicity of the design and the perfect marriage of form and function. The clear glass of the side panels will make the bather appear, and possibly feel, that they are hovering above the ground. Square glass basins are equally intriguing, especially when filled with water as they take on the same visual appeal as a fish tank. The elegant curves of a round glass basin and the sharp edges of a square fitting both have their own unique beauty that will enhance the modern bathroom.

left The interaction between water and glass is always attractive, and so glass is ideally suited for use in the bathroom. This square basin, made by UV-bonding four glass sides to the base, is a modern take on the traditional butler's sink.

right These twin bowls appear to be resting temporarily on the work surface, waiting for the first splash of water from the wall-mounted tap. In fact they are fully functional, with all the plumbing cleverly concealed under the counter, creating a sleek, minimalist wash area.

above This glass bed from Defy Interiors has a glass headboard and footboard attached by metal brackets to acrylic legs – an interesting alternative to wood or metal bed-frames. The look is kept light and fresh with white bedding and pastel accessories.

right In the contemporary glass house there is no room for solid furniture. To maintain the overall sense of space and light in this riverfront home, the owners have chosen a simple white sofa and introduced glass occasional tables that display a few ornaments without distracting from the view.

Moving from the bathroom to the living area, there is certainly no shortage of designs in glass. For example, the use of clear glass for tabletops is nothing new. The German designer Knut Hesterberg created his Propeller table in 1964, using a 19-mm (7/8-in) circular glass top on an aluminium base. The gently twisting base was designed in the shape of a ship's propeller, and appears to be in continuous motion as each of the three angled blades swirls around, one after the other. This unusual table looks as innovative today as it did 40 years ago and it is still produced in Germany by furniture specialists Ronald Schmitt. Yet without its clear glass top, the impact of the Propeller table would be lost.

British designer Tom Schneider is another who has utilized glass, in his case to allow access to the spaces between the wooden supports of his sculptural furniture. He pays particular attention to the spaces between the solid shapes in his designs, and maintains that it is often the shape of the spaces that make the design powerful. There are also designers working purely in glass, and the Ghost chair by Italians Cini Boeri and Tomu Katayanagi (*see* page 2) demonstrates the purity of such designs. There is no texture or colour, nor any additional materials used in this piece to detract from the precise detail of the final form. Although the chair is functional, because it is made entirely from glass it rises above the mundane. The Ghost chair is produced by Fiam Italia from a single thick sheet of hot-curved crystal glass, using a unique high-precision cutting system based on a water jet mixed with abrasive powders that travels at three times the speed of sound.

Glass can be an effective design material, whether it is used as an element within a piece of furniture or as the main component. Clear glass also has the advantage of not clashing with other finishes, working equally well with metal, wood, or plastic. As a result, glass furniture can be incorporated successfully into both traditional and modern interiors, as dining or occasional tables, chairs, display cabinets, and even bedsteads. Clear glass will make a strong impression wherever it is used, but without dominating the interior.

Achieving uninterrupted, see-through architectural designs, from exterior façades and roofs right through to the walls and doors in the centre of a building, is now an achievable reality. Solid roofs, doors, and partitions need no longer block out views or natural light. State-of-the-art glazing can now be used to provide a protected and comfortable environment that also ensures maximum natural daylight and an uninterrupted view. Safety has to be one of the primary considerations when choosing glass as a structural material, and it is vital that the appropriate glass should be specified for the job in hand. Heat-strengthened glass may be preferable to toughened glass, because it cracks, rather than shatters, if damaged. It also has the advantage of being more resistant to localized heat caused by an underfloor light source. Laminated glass not only has added strength but it also holds its shape when broken.

Glass for construction is now put through the most rigorous of tests. Austrian manufacturer Eckelt Glas produces triple-laminate glass that is tested to the German DIN standards, whereby a panel is supported on two edges and a 700-kilo (1,500-lb) weight is placed on top. In order to pass, the glass has to support the weight without buckling for 24 hours. Eckelt Glas takes a force up to 6 kilonewtons a square metre, while the weight of an average person only equates to 1 or 1.5 kilonewtons a square metre.

With increasingly larger spans of glass being specified, it is vitally important that each glass floor installation should be designed to meet its specific loading requirements – this means the number of people or vehicles that will be travelling over the floor. And if it is an outside space, the slip resistance of the floor when wet has to be taken into account in order to avoid slips and falls. Most commonly, glass floor and ceiling panels are fitted on a steel grid to provide support, as opposed to using wooden beams, which are not appropriate as they tend to move. Alternatively, to create the ultimate "clear floor," solid glass beams can be used. Although this increases the cost of a project, it creates an uninterrupted span of glass. While glass isn't the cheapest building material, nothing else can provide the same superb quality of light and space in both commercial and domestic locations.

above The end wall of this home is glass, allowing both bathroom and sleeping area to enjoy the breathtaking view. The simple stairs and wire balustrades have been carefully chosen to complement the determinedly open-plan scheme.

left Architects Foster and Partners created the glass roof covering the Great Court at the British Museum in London. It covers 6,100sqm (7,300sq yards), making this the largest covered open-plan space in Europe.

above Dewhurst MacFarlane installed the glass frontage for Now & Zen. The new façade made the restaurant instantly eye-catching and inviting.

right By choosing to construct the reading room within the Urban Development Institute in Riyadh in glass, Dewhurst MacFarlane were able to create an area in which activity is separated, but not isolated, from the main building.

Engineers Dewhurst MacFarlane pioneered the use of large-span glass floors in the early 1990s, when they set seven 1,100- x 3,900-mm (3ft-7in x 12ft-9in) glass floor plates into the pavement outside the London restaurant Now & Zen. In order to strengthen the glass, two 19-mm (7/8-in) thick glass sheets were laminated together. The design allowed valuable natural light to enter the basement dining room and created a dramatic entrance to the restaurant.

Before this, glass floors had been built using 750-mm (2ft-5in) square tiles, but these had been limited in their visual impact and the amount of light they allowed through. Since the Now & Zen project, the use of large spans of clear glass for floors, stairs, and walkways has become a distinctive feature in new projects such as the Reichstag refurbishment in Germany by Sir Norman Foster in 1995, or the Tokyo International Forum by architect Rafael Vindy in 1996. What is more, technological advances in laminating and strengthening glass now allow even larger and thinner spans of glass to be used. Such developments have ensured that this technique has become an elegant, as well as a practical, alternative to bricks and mortar.

In 1998 Dewhurst MacFarlane worked with Saudi Arabian architects Nabil Fanous to create the glass reading room for the Urban Development Institute in Riyadh, Saudi Arabia. This is an 8-m (26-ft) square glass cube that is housed within the Institute's main building. To create expanses of uninterrupted glass sheets and an impression of fragile clarity, solid structural supports were dispensed with, leaving the roof supported entirely on glass beams with no intermediate columns. Each roof plate measures 900 x 2,700mm (3 x 9ft) and is constructed with two sheets of 15-mm (3/4-in) glass laminated together. The project gained a Special Achievement Commendation at the Institute of Structural Engineers Awards in 1998.

Understandably, safety considerations have to be uppermost in the designer's mind at every stage of a concept involving glass. This can pose construction problems, but the solution almost always lies in the type of glass chosen, or how it is treated to suit the project.

translucent glass

"People have no problem with working behind glass walls as long as those outside can't see who they are. With sandblasted glass you struggle to make out exact shapes, so privacy really isn't an issue." Linda Morey Smith, interior architect   Although transparent walls allow light to flood into the interior, they can also raise issues of privacy. These can be addressed by the use of translucent instead of clear glass – the transparent surface will blur the identities of those behind it, and conceal the detail of their activity without any serious loss of light.

left Swimmers at this pool are protected from the prying eyes of pedestrians on the pavement outside by a waist-high panel of frosted glass. When lit, the panel not only sheds light on the tiled pool edge, but also reflects light back from the water's surface.

The use of glass in interior design can make a space resonate, and yet there are times when its very clarity just isn't suitable. Keen though we might be to open up our living and work spaces, we don't always want to encourage complete visual access to every aspect of our lives. There is a fine line between removing unnecessary barriers and exposing our private spaces to public scrutiny – from the contents of the wardrobe to the places where we dress and bathe. A simple compromise is the use of translucent glass. Semi-transparent, it still allows natural and artificial light to be diffused through it, while also partially obscuring the people or objects behind.

There are several techniques for changing glass from transparent to translucent, the most common being sandblasting. This is a versatile method for etching glass that can be used to create an overall frosted effect or to introduce etched detail, such as logos and graphics. Specialist glass producers can employ sandblasting to create complex, deeply carved, three-dimensional imagery using hand-cut or computer-generated stencils. Once glass has been sandblasted, the treated side does become slightly porous and therefore vulnerable to scuff marks and fingerprints. Architecturally, this is not a problem for floors or stairs where the treated side is unexposed. However, if sandblasted glass is used for walls or screens where people may pass on both sides, it is advisable to have the sandblasted surface treated with a polymer coating that seals and protects the textured work. Sandblasted glass is equally suitable for use in glass furniture and fittings. Dining and coffee tables are also effective when produced in frosted glass, as are shower enclosures and basins, and light fittings, where the light is gently diffused, softening the impact of the electric bulb.

An alternative method of creating translucency is by inserting a secondary material between two sheets of glass. A thin sheet of white plastic sandwiched between two sheets of glass creates a milky finish which can be used for glass-fronted kitchen cabinets or sliding wardrobe doors. And if plastic can be combined with glass, then why not other materials? UK-based decorative glass specialist Fusion has been developing laminated

above The wall of this modern dwelling has been constructed partly from white translucent glass. On the inside, the glass wall rescues the long corridor from being dark; externally, the wall provides light and interest in the garden.

glass panels incorporating an imaginative range of additions, from paper and fine wire mesh to sheer fabric and wood. Fusion's laminated glass can be used for structural and decorative applications, including floors, stair treads, and walls. Glass incorporating a fine wire mesh is virtually transparent but with a silvery spider's web of wire suspended within it. When fabric is introduced as a laminate, it is first soaked in resin so that it bonds to the glass. The sheer fabric, which can be either plain or patterned, creates a completely translucent effect and is an eye-catching alternative to sandblasted glass. Also, because it is laminated on both sides, there is not the risk of the scuffs or smudges associated with sandblasted glass. Microfine wood veneers can also be suspended in the central resin which bonds the glass laminates together, as the veneer is so fine that light still passes through. Fusion has supplied its innovative glass to architectural projects in the UK, USA, and Hong Kong. Director Rob Robertson says, "As far as we know this process is unique: the results are extremely effective, allowing wafer-thin fabric, metal, and even stone to be turned into strong, architectural glass." Introducing a specific fabric or texture into these laminated panels means that they can also be linked with ease to other elements within the interior scheme.

above left A large shower area can be screened from the rest of the bathroom with translucent glass, providing the user with a degree of privacy while still utilizing the natural light from the window.

left The large kitchen in this house has been divided into a preparation and eating area by a long run of white units. A panel of sandblasted glass, back-lit by two spot-lights, breaks up the monotony of the rear view of the units.

Translucent glass is ideal for architectural use because it allows natural light to penetrate deep into a building while maintaining a degree of privacy. For glass stairs and floors the ideal treatment to create translucency is sandblasting. The whole area can be treated or just selected sections, so that there are areas of frosted as well as clear glass. In addition to providing privacy there are other advantages to treating glass floors and stairs in this way. Sandblasting or applying a slightly granular coating to the glass creates a valuable non-slip surface. This treatment also disguises the small scratches that will appear over time on glass surfaces. One supporter of the integration of translucent glass in the office environment is British interior architect Linda Morey Smith, who explains, "It is all to do with the use of natural daylight. A lot of the buildings we work on have a deep space where people might otherwise only have artificial light. Out of choice people would always work next to a window or at least be able to see a window." However, the balance between opening up a building and retaining a level of privacy and client confidentiality does have to be struck. Morey Smith observes, "People have no problem with working behind glass walls as long as those outside can't see who they are."

Glass can be pre-treated to make it translucent prior to installation, either by sandblasting or by inserting a white laminate between two layers of clear glass. There is also a solution for those wanting to change installed clear glass to translucent. Lumisty from Architectural Window Films is a peel-and-stick plastic film that can be applied on site to glass windows and walls. As an alternative to clear-glass or sandblasted floors, British company Cellbond has created the B-Clear range of non-laminated translucent panels, which offer an affordable and versatile variation on traditional glass ones. Constructed with an aluminium honeycomb core and sandwiched between 4-mm (1/4-in) toughened glass, these panels distort images to provide privacy and, because the panels are hollow, can incorporate other features such as a coloured core or fibre optics. B-Clear glass flooring is lighter and stiffer than comparable products, and is available in any size up to 3,000 x 1,500mm (10 x 5ft), with thicknesses ranging from 25mm (1in) to 50mm (2in).

above A light source set into a gully in a polished concrete floor creates the effect of an indoor stream. The gully is then topped with translucent glass panels that lie flush with the floor.

right Large glass doors divide this futuristic home. To add interest to the design, and make the clear glass more visible, a series of large, translucent squares has been sandblasted onto the surface. The pattern echoes the square shape of the aperture.

As an alternative to sheets of translucent glass, glass bricks can be used in an architectural context to create both internal and external walls. Solid glass bricks are cemented together in much the same way as conventional bricks, to create a strong yet transparent wall. Because of the thickness of the individual bricks and the sturdy nature of the final construction, glass-brick walls will stand by themselves and do not need to be set into any supporting framework.

A solid wall can be interspersed with glass-brick sections. This is perfect for exterior construction, as the combination of the two materials allows the wall to be load bearing. Vertical glass-brick sections can be built to the full height of the property, allowing plenty of light in and making a strong visual statement.

Glass bricks often have a slightly rippled surface that helps to provide a degree of privacy. This is enhanced when several bricks are joined together, creating a grid effect. This breaks up and distorts the view through the wall still further, so that although movement and colours are discernible, precise shapes are blurred.

Because of the thickness of the glass used, each brick has a slightly green or blue tint, which is particularly noticeable when either daylight or artificial light shines through. By positioning a light source close behind the wall it is possible to create a warm, glowing effect, with the textured surface of the bricks throwing fascinating shadows on to the surrounding surfaces.

Glass bricks are useful in any situation that requires both a maximum flow of light and a degree of privacy. They might be used to divide two areas of living space, for instance creating a separate dining room from the main seating area, or in a windowless hall or corridor so that light can permeate from adjoining rooms. Because they do not provide complete privacy, glass bricks are not suitable as a wall to a bathroom, but they can be used to create shower cubicles or to screen the toilet from the bath. Glass-brick walls can also look stunning in the contemporary garden, when used to create a private seating area or to wall off a swimming pool. Their durability makes them a practical choice.

above Replacing a section of internal wall with glass bricks means that this previously dark hallway now benefits from a degree of natural light. As glass bricks are quite thick they provide both sound and heat insulation, so the room on the other side of the wall remains unaffected by this change of building material.

left Glass bricks can be used both internally and externally. Here, a two-storey section of the wall has been built using glass bricks. This creates interest around the main entrance to the house and replaces the need for a window.

Translucent glass is an effective material for use within fitted furniture. When used for kitchen cabinet or wardrobe fronts, it breaks up an otherwise solid run of doors without fully exposing the contents. Every home needs some form of clothes storage, yet a large wardrobe can dominate a room. The solution can be to break up the solid mass of the furniture by allowing light to filter through. Because there are few wardrobes whose contents can stand up to clear scrutiny, translucent doors are a practical alternative to fully transparent ones, with only the vaguest outlines of shirts and jackets visible, softening the final look of the storage system and creating interest within the room. Wardrobe systems with sliding translucent panels can be built against a wall or used as a room divider, perhaps separating the sleeping area from the bathroom or creating a self-contained dressing room within the main bedroom.

In the kitchen, frosted glass plays an important role. It can be used as a supplementary material to the main fabric of the kitchen, co-ordinating well with wood, stainless steel, granite, or laminate. As frosted glass is colourless it will not clash with the colour scheme and can be used effectively in both contemporary and traditional settings. If the contents of the cupboards are pushed a little way back from the doors, the exact shapes and labels of the stored items beyond become blurred — even the shape of a jar or the colour of a label can become intriguing when partially obscured. This is also a useful way of introducing a gentle sense of colour into an otherwise monochromatic interior scheme.

The use of frosted glass in the kitchen creates a more open, and less fitted, finish to the room, and even when several cabinets are fitted together the result is not so dominating as if the doors were solid. Perhaps the best quality of translucent glass is the relationship it has with artificial light. Frosted glass softens the effect of electric lights, diffusing the force of the bulb so that the resulting light is much softer. A striking effect can be achieved by installing a light source inside a translucent, glass-fronted cabinet. The unit then takes on a dual role, providing both useful storage and a source of artificial light within the room.

above This simple locker-style cabinet provides ample storage. The contents are faintly visible behind the numbered doors.

right When objects are placed behind translucent glass, outlines become blurred and colours are softened. Gentle lighting enhances the effect, so that even the most everyday item can be displayed effectively.

When used imaginatively for free-standing pieces such as tables and chairs, translucent glass maintains the sharp, striking effect of clear glass furniture, while also endowing the pieces with a more substantial presence. Clear glass within tabletops allows visual access to the shape of the base, acting as a window to the central part of the design, the table support. With a translucent glass tabletop, the balance of the design changes and the tabletop shares equal prominence with the base. A good example of this is the Spiral coffee table from Cattelan Italia. Cut from a single sheet of tempered glass, the spiral top not only curls around itself, but also winds gently down towards the floor. Frosted glass was used for this design in order to enhance the movement of the table with its translucent, almost liquid appearance. The Spiral table would not have been so effective if it had been constructed from clear glass, because the base, rather than the concise shape of the tabletop, would then have been the main feature.

By contrast, it is the complete simplicity of Curvet's Ponte nesting tables that gives them their appeal. The tables consist of a sheet of annealed glass that is bent into a three-sided shape. As the tables are manufactured from a continuous sheet of glass, rather than three bonded sections, it is possible to incorporate gently rounded corners into the design. The tables are available in clear glass, but it is the frosted glass designs that are the most successful. The added dimension and texture of the finish makes the tables much more significant within the room than simply a collection of curved sheets of glass.

Translucent glass is a good material to use for light fittings, whether as wall, pendant, or table lamps. Sandblasted glass is often used for these fittings and the resulting frosted appearance diffuses the artificial light, making it bright enough to light a room, yet softening its harshness. Petra Karsenbarg has created a range of frosted glass light fittings for B Sweden. Bubble, available as a pendant and a table lamp, was created in 2001. The shape is organic, with the glass cylinder swelling at one end around the light source. When switched on, the lamp gently diffuses light through the glass, creating a glowing core that gradually fades at the extremities.

above Translucent glass is perfect for light fittings, as it softens the effect of the light bulb and gently diffuses white light.

left Frosted glass has the advantage of working well with a wide range of other finishes. This kitchen successfully brings together a variety of materials, including brick, wood, stainless steel, and glass, to create a relaxed look.

above Curved, sandblasted glass panels have been used here to create room-height pods within a contemporary living space. One pod houses a basin and toilet, the other a shower. The concept of a separate bathroom has been dispensed with.

The use of clear glass is appropriate in a bathroom because of its strong relationship with water, but translucent glass has a place in the bathroom too. This material may suit those who prefer not to withstand the full exposure of clear glass – particularly when used for baths and shower doors. Translucent glass will still allow light to pass through the installation, while at the same time shrouding the figure inside.

Another reason why translucent glass might be considered for a bathroom is to avoid unsightly watermarks. As soon as water dries on glass it leaves behind a watermark, particularly in hard-water areas. The whole point of clear-glass fittings is that they should be just that – clear. Even the slightest mark will spoil the overall effect. This problem is greatly reduced by using translucent glass – as the surface is not transparent the marks are correspondingly less obvious. It can be most effective when used for shower doors, where a large expanse of glass can quickly become marked. The shower door and side panels need not be completely frosted: a striped or wave pattern will disguise watermarks while also maintaining a level of privacy.

Most shower manufacturers offer both clear and frosted glass options, and some will customize shower doors with specially commissioned sandblasted patterns. There is also the choice of framed or unframed enclosures. Frames for doors and wall sections are usually in aluminium or rigid plastic, the unframed option leaving the cubicle completely clear of fittings other than simple hinges and handles.

Translucent glass basins are widely available, either as inset or countertop designs. An all-in-one glass counter with integral basin will create a clean, crisp finish to the bathroom, making the perfect addition to a modern scheme where plain white ceramic fittings and a glass shower screen have been used. Glass basins are surprisingly easy to clean and extremely hardwearing. As a result, they are being specified increasingly for contract as well as domestic use, providing an attractive and practical solution to the problem of creating stylish bathrooms in clubs and hotels, as well as in the home.

right Sliding doors of frosted glass divide
this en suite bathroom from the main bedroom.
The doors provide privacy for the bather
while giving this small area a much greater
sense of space.

Antoine Raffoul of UK architects Raffoul Darrer called on the services of specialist manufacturers and installers Firman Glass to transform an apartment in London's Notting Hill into a modern bachelor pad. The main structural glass feature was a staircase introduced to give access to a newly created loft room. Raffoul and his client decided to use glass, because they wanted to get as much natural light flowing through the flat as possible. The new staircase, which incorporates fibre-optic lighting, curves around a central column to the room above, while also forming the ceiling of the bathroom. Raffoul Darrer aimed to integrate the staircase as a subtle design feature, because making a staircase the predominant feature is not appropriate for a domestic setting (unlike a corporate commission). Small parts of the stairway can be seen from all over the apartment, but a full view is only possible when you are actually using it.

The bath and shower are positioned underneath the dog-leg turn in the stairs, and yet privacy is maintained as the glass was back-coated with an acrylic film to create a misty finish. Light therefore floods through, but shapes are barely discernible. The stair treads are made from one skin of float glass with a sandblasted texture to give slip resistance, and the front edges have been highly polished to give a contrasting glassy green line against the frosted treads and uprights. The stairs are supported by purpose-made stainless steel bearers and a metal spine. Firman Glass also supplied the bright, polished stainless-steel handrail, designed and manufactured by its architectural metal department. Raffoul notes that although the results are quite dramatic, the installation process was made straightforward because of Firman's expertise. They calculated the angles by creating a template and then working out the exact angles of the treads. The staircase arrived in pieces and Firman built it up bit by bit like a well-planned puzzle. A project such as this really depends on finding a specialist glass contractor who knows how to use the material and can advise on finishes and installation. As with all glass installations, it was important to take into account not only the final look of the staircase, but also how it would be installed, and its final load-bearing capacity.

above Although the bath fits snugly underneath the turn in the stairs, any risk of claustrophobia has been removed as the stairs are translucent. The effect is more like bathing under a window than under a solid structure.

left The staircase incorporates fibre-optic lighting so that it glows in the dark. The central section of each tread has been sandblasted to give a non-slip surface.

"The key element is how light works with the glass: coloured light is just lovely in itself and the way a stained glass window or wall panel throws fragments of colour onto the surrounding walls is fascinating." Kate Maestri, glass artist Coloured glass can be seductively inviting, adding both drama and life to the coldest interior. With clever lighting techniques, blue and green glass become luminescent, while red and orange surfaces glow with smouldering fire.

left The smallest piece of coloured glass can contribute to the rich texture of a home, as with this panel of midnight-blue glass in the door between a dining room and hall.

The idea of glass surfaces in an interior tends to conjure up images of cool, clear glass with reflections in blue and grey, or the frosted effect of sandblasting. But colour is now an inescapable part of the glass palette, and this gives the material a whole new range of decorative applications. The technique of introducing a coloured pigment into glass is centuries old. When Tutankhamun, the Egyptian pharaoh, died in 1323 BC, his mummified body was buried with lavish treasures, and many of these were decorated with coloured glass rather than jewels. In the ancient land of the pharaohs glass was highly prized, and only the kings and their high priests were considered worthy of owning it.

Coloured glass bowls, vases, and ornaments still have a perennial appeal and there are plenty of designers exploiting the rich, jewel-like quality of coloured glass for traditional and contemporary domestic accessories — from dishes to curtain finials, and from decanters to door knobs. Coloured glass is also increasingly being specified for architectural applications. Where walls, floors, and stairs were previously only specified in clear or slightly green-tinted glass, interiors are now being transformed with glass surfaces in vibrant shades of amber, green, and blue. This is largely due to recent advances in technology that have enabled manufacturers to create large sheets of architectural glass in a wide range of standard or custom colours. The use of coloured glass as part of an interior project can be extremely useful as an alternative to translucent glass. Large-span glass can be used as a room divider, allowing light through and creating a dramatic focal point of colour.

Traditionally associated with religious buildings, stained glass is now finding its way into domestic and commercial interiors. The contemporary stained-glass window or wall tends to present an abstract rather than pictorial design, or to combine panels of contrasting colour in geometric patterns. When colour is introduced to a room the mood changes significantly: generally red tones project a feeling of warmth while blue is cool. The key to coloured glass is its interaction with natural and artificial lighting. It not only looks beautiful as light shines through but can also bring a certain magical quality to an interior, creating little flecks and sparks of colour in the room.

There are a number of techniques for adding colour to glass while still maintaining its transparent quality. The oldest method is to add pigment to the glass itself, creating the type of stained glass traditionally used in decorative ecclesiastical windows. This method often results in a slightly uneven distribution of colour that enhances the "antique" quality of the finished glass. Glass can also be painted with enamel colours and then fired to create specific images.

To produce sheets of glass with pure, clear colours, the best method is to create resin laminates. Coloured resin is poured into a small gap between two sheets of glass. Once the resin has set, the edges can be trimmed and polished. This method not only colours but also strengthens the glass, allowing the production of relatively large panels. The resin can be colour matched to a client's specification, so that the glass can be made to co-ordinate with an interior scheme or to feature a particular corporate colour. The depth of colour is dependent on the percentage of pigment used – five per cent pigment would result in a tinted but transparent glass, whereas twenty-five per cent pigment would be much darker. It is also possible to add subtle touches of colour to bonded glass furniture and fittings by introducing colour to the UV resin. Adding dyes to the normally clear resin means that the bonded joint can be highlighted in an almost limitless range of colours. This makes possible the addition of a subtle line of colour to otherwise clear glass furniture, thereby highlighting the horizontal and vertical elements of the piece.

American glass specialist Curvet has developed an exclusive system for colouring glass. Its trademarked Colorglass system offers an infinite number of variations for dramatically changing the appearance of glass, from single-colour transparent glass to opaque or silvered glass, or glass that, with two or more decorative applications, can appear dappled, striped, speckled, or even marbled like stone. The effects are achieved without altering the natural advantages and qualities of the glass. Ozone Glass has also developed Chromazone, its own range of transparent, opaque, and metallic applied colours that can be used with smooth and textured glass.

above Photo images can be laminated onto glass. This simple image of the sea has a mesmerizing effect, as the waves appear to undulate gently, bringing the otherwise stark white interior of the room to life.

left Alternating rectangular panels of dark blue and white glass have created a checkerboard effect in this feature wall. The rooms on both sides of the divide benefit from this installation.

It is believed that the Romans used coloured glass set in lead to form the windows in their houses. The practice of painting designs on to glass that was then fired probably began around the fifth century AD. Stained-glass windows were used primarily for churches, and there are many fine historical examples of this ancient craft.

The various new techniques for colouring glass allow contemporary designers to dispense with the restrictions of setting small coloured glass fragments in lead, and create stronger glass in significantly larger spans for use in architecture. Stained-glass windows, walls, and screens can be used as colourful alternatives to translucent glass. There are also a number of glass artists who create large-scale pieces to specific requirements, depicting both abstract and realistic representations of the surroundings. Andrew Moor has an international reputation as an expert in the field of glass art. His UK company, Andrew Moor Associates, is a project-based architectural glass design consultancy that deals with every stage of design and production from concept to completion. The consultancy has worked with a variety of established and emerging young artists, and projects have ranged from partition screens to a glazed roof light of nearly 1,000 square metres (1,100 square yards). The expertise of this company lies in their ability to make the commissioning of something quite original in glass straightforward, economically viable, and technically feasible.

In 2000 the company worked with the architects The Coleman Partnership on their Notting Hill project Holmes Place, a fashionable London gym and fitness centre. The architects wanted to install a large coloured glass wall at one end of the swimming pool, to screen off the glass stairs beyond. This would allow passers-by to see the swimming pool, while at the same time maintaining privacy for the swimmers. British glass-artist Graham Jones designed the blue-and-green wall, which was manufactured from enamelled and etched flat and antique glass. The wall makes a dramatic statement at the end of the pool: it mirrors the colour of the water below and swimmers can enjoy Jones' work without being viewed by spectators from the stairs. Andrew Moor has seen coloured glass

left Large-scale glass art is undeniably
dramatic. Here glass artist Graham Jones
has screen-printed an abstract pattern onto
many sandblasted glass panels that, when
pieced together, result in a vast wall full of
movement and light.

right Jones also designed this wall for Holmes
Place gym. The two-storey wall is coloured with
splashes of green and blue enamel and screens
the swimmers from the staircase beyond.

glass specified increasingly by architects for use in internal walls, and he attributes this to the industry having pushed technology forward significantly in recent years. Screen-printing and etching have allowed artists to create large-scale glass panels that appeal to architects, because they are used to working with both the material and the scale. So coloured glass is now much easier to combine with modern architectural practice.

Daedalian Glass produces creative glass for architects and designers. With several corporate projects in sandblasted glass behind it, including huge decorative screens for Britain's National Museum of Photography, Film and Television in Bradford in 1999, Daedalian is now introducing coloured elements to its work in glass. Using Diachroic glass, a metallic glass with a coloured coating that changes its hue when viewed from different angles, the company has created some highly imaginative effects. In a corporate project in 2001 for the Phoenix advertising agency, the company created decorative glass panels to disguise a boxed-in spiral staircase that was positioned in the centre of an office. Four glass panels were fitted around the staircase and held top and bottom by metal brackets. The panels were set slightly proud of the wall, allowing a two-dimensional effect to be created from the shadows cast by the design when light shines through it. The inspiration for the design came from organ pipes, as the building was an old church, and from a bird's nest that had been found during renovation. The panels incorporate irregular squares of coloured Diachroic glass. Developed in the USA by the space industry, Diachroic glass is coated in layers of micron-thin metals: these react differently to light, both transmitting and reflecting it at the same time, so that you see complementary colours as you move around the glass. Daedalian has also been working with sheet glass, which it colours on one side; the colour is sandblasted or carved away to create further designs.

These pieces are part of a collection of emerging work from a number of companies, which marks a reawakening interest in the excitement of coloured glass, and moves away from solid colours to the more decorative finishes that can be achieved with techniques such as bonding.

above For high-drama effect, these blood-red glass panels by artist Kirsty Brooks have been lit from behind. Some areas become almost transparent, while others fade from red to black.

left Brooks' black-and-white photographic images set on glass create fascinating screens. The light passing through the glass brings the images to life with a 3D effect.

A less drastic alternative to introducing fully transparent or translucent walls is to clad existing solid walls in materials that are sympathetic with the other glass elements within the room. Coloured glass sheets and tiles, although not fully transparent, have a three-dimensional shimmer, creating colours that glimmer within an interior scheme in a myriad of glassy, clear surfaces.

Sheets of back-coated glass can easily be fixed to walls as a protective splashback behind the bathroom basin or kitchen sink, or to clad an uninspiring wall. Coloured glass tiles are an equally eye-catching alternative, giving the impression of stained-glass windows within solid internal walls. There is a wealth of coloured glass tiles available, made from pigmented glass or with a coloured application to the back surface. Metallic treatments can also be introduced, so that the tiles glow with colour as well as glittering with a metallic sheen. The Natural Tile Company in London produces a contemporary range of tiles that are hand-made in batches, giving them an appealing variety that is not easily imitated by larger producers. Their aim is to remove the predictability that has always been associated with traditional tile-making, and to use alternative materials — such as metal, glass, and resin — and with them to create new traditions. Liquid Fusion is just one stunning range of glass tiles from The Natural Tile Company, produced in a range of jewel-coloured, light-reflective glass. There is a choice of pure colours that includes amber, turquoise, and green, and colour combinations such as blue on turquoise or amber on clear glass. The natural air bubbles that remain trapped in the glass and the transparent quality of the tiles bring them to life. Light seems to bounce through the tiles, making the rich colours glow and creating a depth of colour that is impossible to achieve with the ceramic alternatives. Thin coloured glass tiles can also be used to create a decorative wall feature in both domestic and contract settings. A panel, constructed from a series of pigmented or hand-painted glass squares set into a simple framework, can be fitted in front of an unsightly window or blank wall and then lit from behind. The coloured glass creates a tapestry of colour similar in richness to an intricate embroidery.

left Tiles made from glass are not strictly transparent, but they are more vibrant than traditional flat ceramic. A mosaic of blue and purple glass has been used to clad this fireplace.

right The back wall of this bar is made up of painted glass tiles in co-ordinating shades of burnt orange, gold, and red. As the rest of the décor is virtually black, this decorative backdrop adds a much-needed splash of colour.

We have seen how designers have promoted the idea of glass in the bathroom and how manufacturers have responded with a wide range of clear and frosted basins. As glass becomes more acceptable as a material for both domestic and contract fittings, so we see new shapes and colours emerging. Coloured glass basins still have a transparent quality, so the visual appeal of seeing water through glass remains. The difference is that there is now a choice of rich, glowing colours in bathroom fittings, from deep sapphire-blue to gold, dark green, and purple.

Coloured glass basins are made from toughened glass and have the significant advantage of being easy to clean. They can be surface-mounted on a countertop so that the fittings are concealed or alternatively wall-mounted on metal brackets that become part of the overall design. The use of a coloured glass basin in a bathroom scheme moves the emphasis away from the bath or shower fitting and back to the counter-top. The basin can look equally powerful when empty or in use, and it combines well with both natural and artificial light, casting pools of vibrant colour on the surrounding surfaces.

Bathrooms International's addition for 2001 was a range of glass basins that are designed for countertops. The basins are available in clear, blue, or green-gold glass and each colour is offered in a round or square shape with flat, polished edges. Schott, a bathroom supplier based in Germany, can supply a range of blue glass bowls with stainless-steel brackets and matching taps.

Baths and shower enclosures have long been the dominant feature in the bathroom, but with the advent of elegant glass countertop fittings the focus of attention is being moved firmly to the basin.

Clear and opaque glass basins have proved popular among interior designers for some time. The introduction of coloured glass in such dominant shades as dark blue and green opens up new avenues of creativity in the bathroom, and gives designers further scope for creating a strong, contemporary look. Even the smallest cloakroom or most compact en suite can be given a strong sense of style with dramatic coloured glass fittings.

left A glass basin in sapphire-blue would become the focal point of any bathroom or cloakroom. This simple circular bowl is mounted on the wall with chrome brackets, which are complemented by the high curving spout of the tap.

right Thick slabs of glass take on a faint green tint that only helps to enhance their aquatic appeal. Here, a curved countertop with integral basin has been sandblasted on the reverse side, resulting in an attractive and practical bathroom vanity unit.

Coloured glass accessories have always had an exotic allure. The Egyptians valued coloured glass ornaments almost as much as jewels, and the Romans used pigmented glass for wine decanters and ornate goblets. Throughout history, the decorative quality of coloured glass has been highly prized, and each generation has favoured different fashions in coloured glass, from the pink-tinted Victorian cranberry glass to the bulbous yellow and orange platters and vases of the 1970s.

The current emphasis in coloured glass accessories is on subtle, simple designs. Shapes are smooth and fluid, and colours are strong and incorporated into clear or untextured glass. The British company McKinney & Co. has produced a range of glass finials so that the transparent theme can be carried right through to the curtain pole. They feature a central mass of coloured glass, giving them the appearance of chunky paperweights.

First Glass is the dynamic, young, London-based partnership of Bob Crooks and Stewart Hearn. Their philosophy revolves around glassware that is innovative, sometimes provocative, and always challenging. Their work encompasses all aspects of hand-made decorative and functional pieces, from tableware to larger unique objects such as suspended plates and lighting. The pair work independently of each other, but their individual pieces complement each other well. They aim to escape the restrictions of factory-made glass, so all the pieces are hand-blown and hand-finished using traditional techniques, and they avoid the use of glass moulds. While the techniques are traditional, the results are modern. Bob Crooks' Spiralae decanters typify the company's philosophy. These rainbow bright pieces feature two contrasting colours – blue and green, or pink and orange – with an additional colour thread. The shapes are smooth with elongated stoppers – a complete contrast to the traditional, clear, cut-crystal decanters.

Crooks and Hearn maintain that, "Glass has been promoted as the material of the future for the past five years: in fact it will probably continue to break new ground for the next fifteen."

above Glass holds colour extremely well, from the palest pastels to deep, vibrant shades. This chunky artwork from Kate Maestri uses slabs of glass in shades of green, mounted in a clear Perspex frame.

left As an alternative to fabric blinds, rectangles of decorative glass have been fixed across the windows of this stairwell. A milky-white laminate has been applied to the glass to make it translucent, while interest is added in the form of a pink and red frieze.

London-based architectural glass artist Kate Maestri works to private and corporate commissions and on large-scale public art projects. Her innovative use of contemporary stained glass offers new possibilities for architectural and domestic spaces. Central to her work is the changing interaction between light sources and coloured glass – in particular the way that light shining through coloured glass will create mesmerizing, shifting, pools of colour within the location. Her distinctive interior glass wall panels can also be used as lighting installations.

Maestri uses different techniques for her pieces, including screen-printing on glass with fired-on ceramic enamels and antique stained glass, which is glass created using the traditional method of blowing coloured glass on tin sheets. The antique glass has a slightly uneven quality and surface texture and retains many small air bubbles. Maestri also uses a technique of bonding strips of coloured glass onto a glass sheet, and mounts chunks of coloured glass in a Perspex housing. She likes to be familiar with the latest glass technology to ensure that her pieces are pushing the boundaries of possibility. The bonding and screen-printing techniques that she uses actually dispense with the need for the lead that makes traditional coloured glass look so heavy. Maestri tends to use varying shades of a single hue in her individual pieces, particularly blues and greens, as these create an atmosphere of tranquillity. She explains that, "The colour is the important element and I want it to appear as if it is floating." This is one of the reasons that she uses antique glass – the colours are so extensive that there are as many as 50 different shades of blue available.

Her recent London commissions include a glass ceiling for The Royal London Hospital NHS Trust, the entrance hall to Morgan Stanley Dean Witter's headquarters, and a glass light installation for J D Wetherspoon at Canary Wharf. Maestri designs with the urban environment in mind – her angular, linear pieces echo the contemporary, functional architecture of the city. Clean lines, glowing colours, and minimal designs are the hallmarks of Maestri's work, which creates light and tranquillity in built-up environments.

above Strips of contrasting colour have been screen-printed onto blue glass panels to create this large, curved installation in an otherwise sombre room. The coloured strips, in red, green, and pale blue, leap from one panel to the next to create a sense of continuous movement.

right Maestri likes to use several shades of the same colour in her work. Here, strips of blue glass in vertical stripes make up a three-panelled screen.

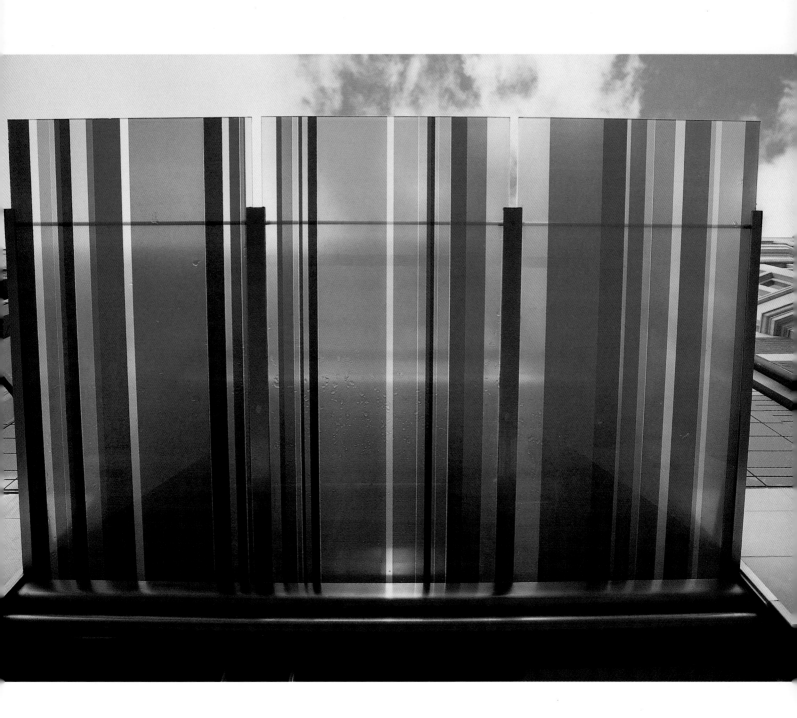

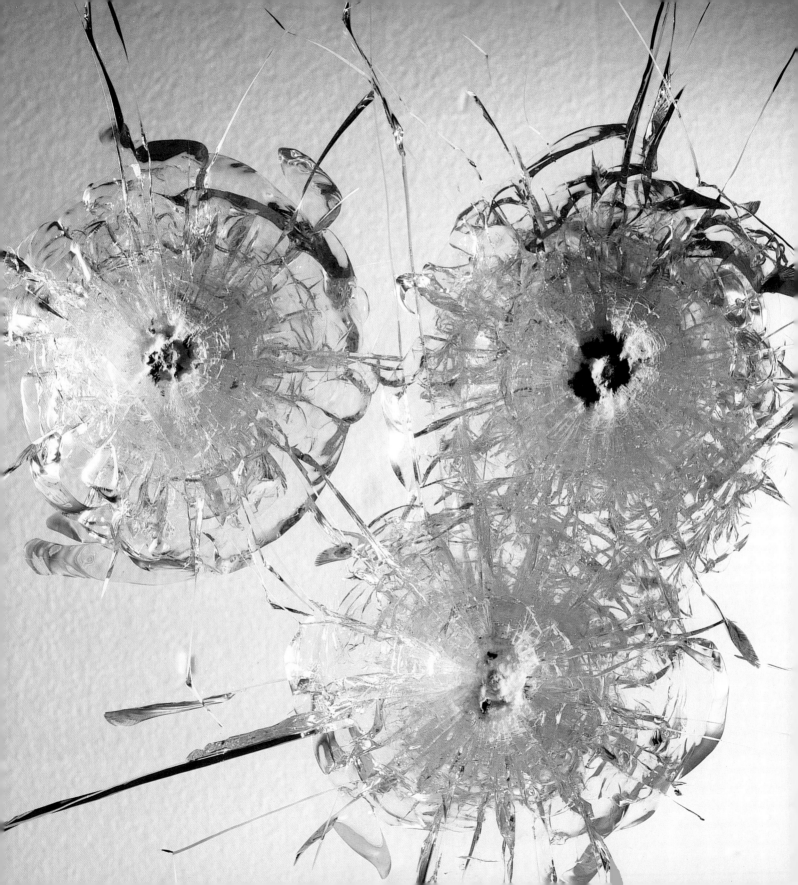

textured glass

"It's the final texture of my work that really appeals to me. You can never predict what it will

finally look like, so many little bubbles and fine details appear to make each piece individual."

Jo Downs, glass artist   Textured glass is a fascinating design paradox. Ever since glass was first

created, the aim has been to produce the smoothest, most flawless results. So to introduce bubbles

and ridges intentionally seems almost perverse. However, these contrived imperfections give glass

a natural appeal, creating the impression of rippling water or chunks of glacial ice.

left The floral bursts on this clear pane of glass have been caused by intentionally damaging
the surface. The damage is controlled to create a pattern without losing the strength of the glass.

Glass does not always have a smooth, flat surface, but can also be quite heavily textured. Texture can be introduced to glass by using a technique called deep-etched sandblasting, in which the surface of the glass is cut away. This method can be employed to replicate detailed designs using stencils, thus creating patterns or displaying a particular logo or image. A three-dimensional effect can also be achieved by increasing the depth of the blasting. The disadvantage of sandblasting is that the roughened glass is susceptible to dirt, so it may show greasy marks and fingerprints in a short time. This can be overcome by installing the glass with the sandblasted surface at the back of the panel, so that while the texture can be seen, the surface of the piece is still flat.

There are other methods for creating textured glass that also allow the textured surface to be directly on display and to be handled. Kiln casting is a technique where the glass is formed over moulds that create textures and patterns in the surface of the glass. The resulting glass sheets have rich, fluid textures that can be toughened or laminated for internal and external glazing, and are ideal for partitions, cladding, balustrades, and floors. One side of the kiln-cast sheets is smooth and the other is textured. However, unlike sandblasted glass, the textured side has a smooth finish and is therefore less likely to show smudges and far easier to clean. Kiln-cast glass can be used with either the flat surface or the textured surface to the front. This glass is available in standard designs, or it can be customized to meet specific requirements. As with all float glass, kiln-cast glass can be coloured or have a decorative laminate applied to the surface.

Another method of creating a textured finish is to fuse layers of glass together. A selection of glass shapes is stacked one on top of the other and then heated just enough to fuse them without melting them into one lump. Although this is a far more labour-intensive method, the results can be dramatic, particularly if different-coloured layers are used. The concept of deliberately introducing an irregular surface to glass may initially have seemed odd, but manufacturers such as Ozone and artists such as Jo Downs have created such stunning results that textured glass is now highly valued.

above The shower screen is made of a single panel of textured glass, which provides a contrast to the clear glass roof of this bathroom.

right Water runs down the already rippled surface of these glass panels in an eye-catching corporate installation. The water soaks into a concealed trough and is then pumped round again.

above Jo Downs created the bubbling blue glass panels for this central feature on the P&O cruise liner *Arcadia*. The waved texture and blue glass follow an ocean theme.

right The ribbed green glass floor in this home creates an instant visual impact and reflects natural light from above. It takes on a new dimension at night, when the floor is lit from underneath.

Since the production of glass began, manufacturers have constantly struggled to create the smoothest and most faultless glass possible. It therefore seems somewhat perverse that one of the latest trends in architectural glass is towards textured, non-uniform designs. The beauty of textured glass lies in its glacial quality. Light readily passes through the glass and appears to glow from within, while solid or moving objects behind the glass are completely distorted. Colourless or green-tinted glass is perfectly suited to such textured surfaces, as the lack of colour highlights the organic appearance of the textured surface. Textured glass is also eminently practical, providing surface interest, slip- and dirt-resistance, and privacy.

From partitions to cladding, and from balustrades to flooring, kiln-cast glass is delicate and translucent, yet tough enough to be used structurally. It has only become possible to fire large sheets of glass (up to 2,700 x 1,500mm/9 x 5ft) in the last ten years, so designers and architects are still experimenting with the potential of the material. British company Fusion, specialists in architectural and decorative glass, have developed a standard range of kiln-cast glass in a variety of designs — from ridges and pebbled effects to random criss-cross patterns reminiscent of cracking ice. Fusion's textured glass is available in thicknesses from 6mm ($\frac{1}{4}$ in) up to 25mm (1in), and it can be toughened or laminated. Fusion will also incorporate drill holes and polish the edges of the sheets if required.

Kiln-casting glass is an extremely useful method of customizing glass to suit its environment. Shapes of shells and sea life can be incorporated into the surface for panels that are going to be used in the bathroom, and a rippled effect moulded into the surface forms the perfect backdrop for glass used in a water feature. Alternatively, a geometric pattern of grids and squares will complement the modern urban interior. As well as producing their own standard ranges of kiln-cast glass, specialist manufacturers can tailor their glass to suit the client's interior requirements.

Coloured laminates applied to the surface of the glass can also create dramatic effects. Another idea is to apply a mirror finish to the back surface of the glass — this means that while it still appears transparent, the glass is actually opaque, and light is reflected back from it rather than shining through. These mirror-back panels are useful in interior projects for disguising unsightly elements of the building, such as concrete pillars or a blank wall. Texture is added to the scheme, light is bounced back into the room, and the overall effect is one of large areas of visual activity instead of the flat surface of utility. Textured glass has also been used as balustrades for walkways or even as large, free-standing sculptures. As the glass is cast rather than sandblasted it is resistant to dirt, allowing it to be touched without leaving fingerprints. And the textured surface means that it does not show watermarks.

An alternative to sandblasting and kiln-casting glass is the technique of fusing. This is not the cheapest alternative, as the process is lengthy and labour intensive, but where a particularly distinctive piece of glass is required, fused panels can be unusual and dramatic. British designer Jo Downs has spent years perfecting the process of fusing to create her particular style of textured glass. In simplified terms, she creates sheets of subtly coloured and textured glass, cuts them into shapes, layers them, and then heats them in a kiln just long enough to fuse them gently together. The resulting bubbling sheets can be used for screens, windows, tiles, or cladding that she makes to order, alongside a range of bowls and tableware. Despite the coloured layers, Jo Downs' glass is translucent. Sheets of her bubbling, royal-blue glass have been used as ceiling panels in P&O's cruise liner *Arcadia* and to clad a wall in the reception hall of the Park Hilton Hotel in Munich. This fused glass successfully combines three of the most attractive properties of glass – colour, translucency, and texture.

As the method for creating large sheets of textured glass is still in its relative infancy, it has yet to be seen exactly what dramatic effects can be achieved by incorporating this particular material into our living and working environments. However, designers and manufacturers are constantly developing new ideas to meet the demands of architects determined to exploit fully its beauty and flexibility, and without doubt the use of coloured and textured glass as an alternative to clear glass is on the increase.

left Slick, smart and arctic bright, these walls have been clad on two levels with frosted, textured glass panels lit from above and below. The highly polished metal used for the stairs bounces the light back.

right First impressions count. The feature wall behind this bar has been constructed from a jumble of Ozone textured glass panels in varying sizes, with displays of chilled miniature vodka bottles.

right For more intimate dining, this restaurant installed panels of Ozone textured glass to screen tables from the reception area. The glass has also been laminated, allowing a degree of light to filter through.

Australian glass specialists Ozone claim to be the world's pre-eminent manufacturer of textured glass for architecture, producing a broad range of innovative, formed-glass products for both interior and exterior applications. Ozone produce a standard range of textured glass designs, and project-specific designs are also available that can be produced as originals or on a multiple basis. The company has six different body colours of glass to work with, although the clear float glass that has a slightly green colour is by far the most popular choice. Opaque and translucent colours can then be applied in small areas, as well as other treatments such as sandblasting, metallic colouring, and mirroring.

Ozone offer two distinct textured ranges. Their Originals range, brought out in 2000, includes random-cracked and waved designs plus more figurative leaf and marine patterns. Minimals, brought out the same year, is a clean contemporary range of refined, minimal textures. Both ranges are produced in 10-mm (1/2-in) glass as a standard, but they can be ordered in thicknesses from 6mm (1/4 in) to 25mm (1in). The maximum panel size is 2,700 x 1,400mm (8ft 10in x 4ft 7in). Holes, flat spots, cutouts, and glazing borders can all be incorporated as necessary. Ozone glass can also be toughened, making it five times stronger than conventional glass and therefore suitable for most architectural applications – from stairs and partitions to shower screens and worktops.

For the five-star Regal Hotel at Chep Lap Kok, the airport in Hong Kong, Ozone supplied 1,200- x 1,600-mm (3ft-11in x 5ft-3in) sheets of horizontally textured Dunezone glass to clad the vast pillars in the reception area to a height of 7.20m (23ft 7in). The Concrete columns were first clad in reflective mirror sheets to bounce light back through the glass, and the glass was pin-fixed to the pillars to allow maximum light penetration. The resulting effect is of huge, brightly-lit ice pillars that look decorative and fragile, and successfully disguise the structural nature of the original columns, "From the moment you see it, you'll want to touch and feel it," says the company. Textured glass, especially when cleverly lit, has a tactile appeal that invites you to come up close to look and feel.

If there is one thing that the first few chapters of this book have shown it is the versatility of glass. Not only can it be made strong enough for use as an architectural material for floors and stairs, it is also a fragile, decorative material for lampshades and ornaments. Glass can be coloured, textured, clear, or translucent and can be moulded into a variety of intriguing shapes.

There are two methods of moulding glass. Sheets of glass can be set over the shape they are to emulate and then kiln-heated so that the sheet glass softens and bends; this creates durable shapes such as curved glass chairs or coffee tables. Glass can also be set in moulds, traditionally used to mass-produce glassware such as wine glasses, mixing bowls, and vases. Moulds can be used to create original pieces too, such as glass sculptures. These have the potential to form tactile chunks of solid or hollow glass that, because of their transparent quality, hardly seem there at all.

Daedalian has been experimenting with moulded glass and has produced a range of modern decorative pieces for the commercial interior. One of the company's most successful designs is a giant set of glass cutlery and a plate for the Whitehouse Restaurant in Prestbury, England. After a lengthy process involving clay, rubber, and wax to make the final plastic mould, Davia Walmsley at Daedalian finally had a suitable mould to cast a 1-m (3-ft) knife, fork, and plate in clear glass. These pieces have been hung on the wall at the restaurant: the installation tends to intrigue and draw in the observer, and only at a near distance can you distinguish the flecks of colour and gold leaf suspended within them. Daedalian has subsequently been commissioned to create giant glass cutlery for the British ASK chain of restaurants, and a wonderfully fragile glass eggshell for the Radison SAS hotel. Walmsley predicts that such art within restaurants will be in high demand. As the public becomes ever more discerning, restaurants are responding by displaying specially commissioned pieces on their walls.

As well as making large-scale artwork, glass can be moulded into more practical yet still eye-catching items, such as barrel-shaped stools and coffee tables made from setting liquid glass in a plastic mould, or large upturned hollow containers on metal supports that can be used as bench seating.

above Daedalian Glass created this glass sculpture for the Radison SAS hotel. The fine moulded shape depicts a broken eggshell complete with jagged edges and cracked sides.

right A modern alternative to the wooden bench, here glass has been moulded into courtyard seating for an office.

Glass is surprisingly resilient. It doesn't scratch easily and it is load-bearing, water-repellent, and heat-resistant — all essential qualities for a worktop. Glass is also an accomplished co-ordinator and it never clashes with other materials. A glass worktop would look equally good in a glossy black lacquered kitchen as it would against cherry wood or beech. It is also a material that can easily be combined with other elements, so that sections of the kitchen could be delineated with granite or wooden worktops, with stretches of glass in other areas.

Textured glass should be used for worktops, with the textured surface facing down towards the floor and the smooth side uppermost. The texture of the glass makes it more visible, so it would work well on a projecting or island unit. In addition, the mottled, light-refracting surface does not show spills and smears as obviously as clear glass. Glass worktops are also hygienic, as the completely smooth surface contains no faults or cracks to harbour germs — unlike tiled or wood surfaces. Tabletops and shelving should use 10-mm (1/2-in) thick glass sheets and kitchen worktops and splash backs should use 15-mm (3/4-in) thick sheets.

Sheets of textured glass can be supplied direct from the manufacturer, and there are also specialist worktop makers who can precision-cut the glass to specific shapes and install the worktops on site. Glass can be used as the main worktop over the base units, or as an extension piece with metal leg supports. This method makes more of a feature of the worktop and allows the maximum play of light through its surface. Glass worktops are equally practical in the bathroom, where the theme can be continued with splash backs and shelves. A glass or ceramic basin can be mounted on top of the worktop, or alternatively a glass worktop with integral basin can be created by moulding sheet glass. This looks most effective and is also entirely practical, and easy to clean. In the commercial market glass-topped reception areas and bars can become the main focal point of a room, especially if fibre-optic lighting is incorporated within the installation to enhance the translucent quality of the glass.

above Watermarks don't show as much on textured glass basins and worktops as they do on clear glass. This glass top has been moulded into shape to include an integral basin and small up-stand.

right A large chunk of ridged glass contrasts with the clear glass wall and acts as a screen, while the design is sympathetic to the water feature outside. The textured surface of the glass plays with and distorts the light.

With the application of intense heat, glass sheets can be laid over moulds and bent into shapes to create pieces of occasional furniture. Specialist glass manufacturers Fiam Italia memorably demonstrated this with their Ghost chair, a comfortable armchair formed from a single sheet of clear glass (*see* page 2). Fused and moulded glass can also be used to create pieces of furniture that, while being less transparent, are often softer and more organic in shape.

The Konx coffee table, produced by Fiam Italia, was designed by Ron Arad. The table is manufactured from a sheet of 10-mm (1/2-in) thick fused glass and features six hollowed areas that have been silver-backed. The main part of the table is transparent, giving further dominance to the cratered surface that rests on matt stainless-steel adjustable legs. The company prides themselves on creating curved-glass masterpieces that have a place in the domestic sphere, as well as in museums and public spaces. Fiam Italia has regularly employed the expertise of some of the world's foremost designers to create stunning pieces in glass. Combined with the company's technological expertise and strength of imagination, this has resulted in them enjoying an international reputation for innovative furniture design. Vittorio Livi founded Fiam Italia in 1973, with the aim of freeing "... glass from its historical role as an ornamental accessory and [making] it a protagonist in furnishing."

For the perfect finishing touches in the glass-dominated interior, consider using glass textiles. Suitable for wall hangings, room dividers, and contemporary window treatments, textiles featuring glass have an exquisitely fragile quality. British textile artist Ruth Spaak produces constructed surfaces for interiors using kiln-formed glass shapes that are woven together with industrial fixings in metal or plastic. The mixed media surfaces diffuse light and create exotic shadows and patterns. Spaak ties, knots, weaves, sews, and threads the specially produced glass lozenges and squares in rows, often using coloured plastics, so that the resulting designs are textural and vibrant. The open-weave nature of her work lets virtually all the light through and works with it to create a glittering result.

above Kiln-cast glass can incorporate distinct ridges and geometric shapes, or simply a gently undulating texture, as with this dining table. The texture is on the underside of the table so that the exposed surface remains smooth.

left This bathroom basin is made from clear, moulded glass with a coiling pattern on the reverse side. Plumbed into a tiled worktop, the basin has the appearance of an upturned shell.

"Perspex has a magical property: clearer than crystal it creates optical illusions and is full of many unpredictable surprises."   Jona Hoad, lighting designer   Acrylic sheet has been so universally adopted by designers that brands such as Perspex and Plexiglas have become household names. Plastic may have been invented as a cheap alternative to costly natural materials, but its diverse possibilities and unique flexibility have now positioned it as the material of choice for many designers.

left It looks just like glass, but glass would be too heavy for this quirky chair. The seat is a rectangular block of acrylic, deliberately moulded to have an uneven surface and to include random air bubbles.

Although plastics are thought of as a modern invention, natural polymers such as amber, tortoiseshell, and horn have long been used in the decorative arts. Historically, these natural materials have been used in much the same way as manufactured plastics are today, made into buttons and decorative ornaments or vessels for drink and food. They have been polished, drilled, and carved to suit their function, just as their plastic counterparts are today.

It was the search to find a replacement material for the ivory used to make billiard balls that led to the first man-made plastics. The American Hyatt Brothers developed a process for manufacturing a cellulose nitrate composition, which led to the production of Celluloid, patented in 1870. Although successful for making billiard balls and dental plates, Celluloid was limited in its uses because of its flammability.

It was not until 1907 that the first completely synthetic man-made substance was developed by Leo Baekeland, a chemist from New York. He created a liquid resin, Bakelite, which rapidly hardened to hold the shape of its container. Because Bakelite neither melted nor dissolved, as some of its predecessors did, and it was shatterproof and electrically resistant, it was rapidly accepted for both domestic and military applications, from telephones to weaponry.

As the century progressed, the world saw manufactured polymers taking the place of natural materials such as bone, ivory, and tortoiseshell, which were in short supply. With the advent of the space race in the 1960s, plastics became fashionable. Used in space technology for their lightness and versatility, plastics developed rapidly. Plastic was now used in a range of innovative new products, from clothing to furnishings. No longer considered a cheap alternative to luxury, natural materials, it was employed for its own sake. For example, this period saw the first use of transparent acrylic for furniture and lighting. Since then the use of plastic for interior furnishings has continued to grow, so that it now has a presence at every level of the market, from simple moulded plastic garden tables to cutting-edge transparent Perspex chairs.

All plastics start with crude oil. This is distilled to yield naphtha, which is the crucial element in their production. Different plastics have different polymer chain structures that determine their particular physical characteristics. There are several hundred different plastic polymers, and each one has a combination of properties that makes it suitable for specific applications.

There are two main types of plastics. Thermoplastics, such as acrylic and PVC, can be repeatedly softened and hardened by heating without any appreciable change in their properties. Thermosetting plastics, such as polyurethane and epoxy resin, are initially soft, but set hard after heating and cannot be softened again. Acrylic is ideal for use in furniture design, as it can be heated and bent into shape. Polyurethane is better suited for use in protective coatings and varnish.

One of the advantages of plastic is that it is extremely durable, and does not corrode or decompose. Yet this is also one of its main disadvantages, as it cannot be destroyed; in most cases it emits toxic fumes when burned, resulting in environmental waste problems. Some biodegradable plastics have been developed, but their expense limits their use in manufacture.

One solution to the waste problem is recycling, and a number of designers have risen to the challenge by conjuring up innovative uses for other people's rubbish. The British company Smile Plastics manufactures sheets of recycled plastic for use as furniture or cladding for interior walls. One of their clear plastic sheets incorporates another waste product – shredded, discontinued currency. London company Electrickery specializes in recycling, and has used printed circuit boards to create a range of table lamps.

The next few pages examine a range of different plastics, and illustrate how designers have been working with their unique properties to develop furniture, bathroom fittings, and lighting, as well as cladding and screens suitable for architectural use. When used imaginatively, plastic shrugs off its cheap-and-cheerful image and becomes a viable alternative to more conventional materials, such as glass, ceramic, and wood.

above Vibrant plastics are being used increasingly to incorporate colour. The stand for this glass-topped table is adorned with a vibrant red spiral cut out of a single sheet of acrylic.

left Lengths of pink PVC make up the back and seat of this chair. PVC is a pliable plastic that yields under pressure, which makes the chair comfortable to use rather than rigid.

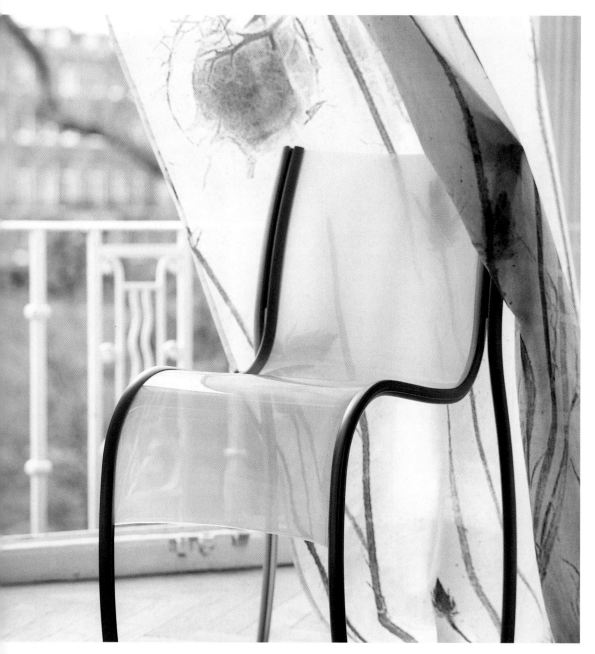

right Acrylic is both tough and lightweight, properties that have been fully exploited in the creation of this suspended chair. The user would have the sensation of relaxing in a huge floating bubble.

left Plastic furniture is no longer regarded as a purely cheap and functional option. Classic designs, such as Ron Arad's FPE chair using translucent white acrylic on a metal frame, prove just how stylish plastic furniture can be.

right A modern take on traditional wooden shutters, these folding screens are made out of two sheets of white acrylic with simple metal hinges. They can be used to provide privacy or diffuse harsh sunlight.

Acrylic is the most widely used plastic for interior products. A tough, lightweight plastic, it can be either transparent or translucent, and combines properties such as surface hardness and excellent weathering ability with high tensile strength while being able to transmit light.

Acrylic sheet is available in a variety of thicknesses, sizes, effects, and colours and can easily be treated by manufacturers with a process known as thermoforming, which involves heating the acrylic sheet and forming it into shapes. It is suitable for furniture, bathroom fittings, and lighting, as well as architectural and industrial applications such as retail point-of sale-displays, screening, and glazing. Acrylic is so widely used that various brand names have now become household names. Throughout Europe acrylic sheet is often referred to as Perspex, while in the USA it is known by the brand name Plexiglas.

Transparent acrylic is valued by designers and manufacturers for its purity. The sheets are faultless and completely lacking in colour and, because acrylic is synthetic, are also consistent in quality. Clear acrylic has a fascinating optical quality – light passes straight through it and appears only on the edges of the sheet. This property has been exploited by a number of furniture and lighting designers to make modern pieces that seem to radiate light.

However, just as designers have been exploring the use of colour and texture in glass, there is now a move to add a further dimension to designs in acrylic. It can be sandblasted like glass to create patterns, or it can be coloured to create subtle or vibrant effects. More intricate, colourful designs or corporate logos can be achieved by screen-printing. Adding colour or a surface finish to acrylic does not take away from the material's light-enhancing qualities, and it opens up new creative avenues for the furniture or interior designer.

Perspex is available in 55 standard colours and an almost limitless range of custom colours. The standard range includes vivid primaries, subtle natural shades, light-diffusing opals and delicate pastel tints that all look as good illuminated as they do in natural daylight.

Acrylic sheet can be used in exactly the same way as glass for interior screens and dividing walls. It is transparent, easy to shape, easy to clean, and durable. It is also lighter than glass and less breakable. However, it is not strong enough to be load-bearing, and the surface is more prone to abrasion marks. Acrylic can be sandblasted to create a degree of privacy between rooms or offices. With the addition of a few simple horizontal or vertical lines, the images beyond the wall can be partially obscured.

Glass is often the first choice for architectural applications because of its more prestigious connotations. However, the use of acrylic panels is on the increase, not just because acrylic is cheaper, but because its man-made, hi-tech image is often more appropriate to the ultra-modern environment.

As well as being suitable for the office interior, acrylic is the perfect material for the retail environment. It is widely used for shop signage as well as display shelves and point-of-sale units. Because of its flexibility, acrylic sheet can be custom-coloured, cut, and shaped to meet the precise demands and image of every retail environment. There are ranges of acrylic products that have been manufactured specifically for retail use. Perspex Frost, for instance, is a double-sided anti-reflective material ideally suited for free-standing, double-sided display units, space dividers, shelving, and brand promotions.

Acrylic sheet can also be used effectively in the domestic interior. Milky-white acrylic panels, set in a wood or metal frame, are ideal for creating room dividers with sliding doors. The acrylic is light enough to let the doors run smoothly, translucent enough to provide privacy, and thin enough to let plenty of light flow through.

Designer Jonathan Forster, of London-based company Forster Inc., used this method to great effect on a recent domestic interior. One wall of the bathroom was replaced with a curved white acrylic sheet set in an industrial-looking metal frame. Oblongs of orange, yellow, and red gel sheets suspended within the acrylic add colour, and a neon light running along the base radiates through the wall, making it glow.

left Acrylic sheet can be used in much the same way as glass to create interior walling. Forster Inc. walled off the bathroom in this flat with translucent acrylic wrapped around a metal frame.

right Coloured gel sheets of red and yellow are suspended within an acrylic wall, which, combined with the grid effect of the metal supports, creates the effect of a painting by the Dutch artist Mondrian.

Clear acrylic was first used in furniture design in the 1960s, when plastic furniture became fashionable. Up until then, transparent acrylic sheet had been associated only with safety glazing and lighting.

The Contour chair, designed in 1970 by UK designer David Colwell, is one of the best examples of transparent plastic furniture. Its transparent acrylic shell (available in clear or smoked) is hand-stretched from a heated flat acrylic sheet and mounted on a stainless-steel frame. The chair was featured in the Modern Chairs exhibition at the Whitechapel Gallery, London in 1970, after which the Victoria and Albert Museum in London purchased two examples. The mouldless forming adopted by Colwell meant that impressive designs could be produced without prohibitive tooling costs.

The fascination with forming acrylic sheet into seating is still very much alive today. Danielle Roberts won the UK New Designer of the Year Award 2001 and the Designers Guild Award 2001 for her acrylic seating. Roberts first screen-prints a design onto a chunky Perspex sheet, which is then heated and bent to create the final shape. She says initial problems arose because the coloured ink cracked when heated and the printed design distorted when bent. She now uses flexible, oil-based ink and her resulting furniture maintains a simplicity of shape while still appearing extremely decorative.

Italian manufacturer Kartell has done much to make plastic furniture desirable. Founded in 1949 by designer Giulio Castelli, Kartell now has a range of seemingly mundane items that are incredibly covetable. Castelli's vision was to make plastic aesthetically pleasing, a philosophy continued by the company with pieces designed by, among others, Ron Arad and Philippe Starck. The range includes folding acrylic stepladders in glowing red, yellow, or blue by Alberto Meda and the clip-together Infinity wine rack in translucent acrylic by Arad. One of the most popular designs in the range is One, a collection of stackable containers designed by Piero Lissoni and Patricia Urquiola in satin-finish translucent acrylic with an aluminium frame. This versatile design is available in five subtle colours, including yellow, orange, and grey, and can be fitted with sliding doors, wheels, or feet to provide simple yet highly versatile storage.

above The transparent chairs and table in this kitchen prevent the room from appearing too cramped. A solid dining set would have swamped the small space.

left It looks as modern today as it did in 1970. Contour, by David Colwell, is made by stretching a hot sheet of transparent acrylic over the square metal chair frame. It is simple but extremely effective.

The versatility of acrylic means it does not have to be used only as sheet for screens or dividing walls, or cut and bent into pieces of furniture. An alternative method for manufacturing furniture is to set acrylic in moulds, which creates some very different results.

The Italian company Sturm und Plastic has developed a unique range of moulded acrylic furniture which, once seen, is not easily forgotten. To create its particular look, liquid acrylic is poured into aluminium moulds and, just before it finally sets, air is blown into the shapes to create random bubbles. The resulting furniture has an ice-like quality, with a seemingly liquid core. The tiny air bubbles and faults appearing in the colourless, transparent material give each piece an individual character, while light bouncing through the acrylic creates figures and shadows within.

This process has been used to create a wide range of furniture, from simple acrylic blocks, strong enough to be used in walls or floors, to chairs and tables. The Bloody Mary chair, designed by RaRi, has a conventional dining-chair shape with a panel of air-blown acrylic forming the seat and back. In contrast, the doughnut-shaped Human Being chair, designed by Pascal Bauer, is made from a single piece of moulded acrylic for the circular seat, which looks soft and pliable but is in fact rigid. The seat is set on four metal legs, and would work well in a contemporary bar area. The On The Rocks range of tables, designed by Gigi Rigamonti, has a chunky slab top which appears to teeter on legs made from giant ice cubes. The cubes are set deliberately at angles to add to the precarious effect. Smaller items such as picture frames, shelving units, and lights have also been created using this method.

Sturm und Plastic furniture has an overwhelmingly tactile appeal. It looks cold and smooth, even brittle, and demands to be touched. The company says customers are often intimidated by the furniture because it looks so fragile, but when they realize the items are made from solid plastic, and they feel the weight of the pieces, they are quickly reassured.

Because acrylic is so resilient and easy to clean, the Sturm und Plastic range is ideal for contract applications where a modern or themed area is being created.

above Three acrylic cubes are stacked one on top of the other to create the legs for this table, appropriately named On The Rocks. The table is solid but intentionally precarious looking because the cubes sit at odd angles to each other.

right The circular Human Being seat is supported on three metal legs. The acrylic has taken on all the folds and wrinkles of its original mould and looks as soft and pliable as a rubber ring.

left Glo-nuts from BoBo are made out of
Perspex acrylic in the Frost range of colours.
The illuminated forms can be stacked on the
floor or wall-mounted, and have a variety of
uses, from seating to lighting.

right A thin sheet of red acrylic is wrapped
round itself and fixed on to a wooden base
for this tabletop light from Lampholder 2000.
The light bulb glows brightly at the base of
the lamp, fading from white through yellow
to red at the extremities.

Transparent acrylic sheet has a dramatic optical quality. Light passes straight through it but appears to glow out from its edges. This effect has been used in furniture design, where chairs and tables made from thermoformed acrylic seem to radiate light round the edges, and it is a quality that can be exploited fully in contemporary light fittings.

London designer Jona Hoad used Perspex for his Simply Clear range of lights. Light is directed up through chunky 45-mm (1 3/4 -in) thick Perspex sections, but appears only on the edges of the piece. Hoad explains, "I am fascinated by the idea of manipulating light. Perspex is so clear, light passes straight through, only being held on the frosted surface. People find it intriguing." Although Hoad's lights are powerful enough to read by, he says many people buy them purely for their sculptural quality. The lights look good on their own or a number of them can be grouped together for greater effect. Hoad says, "Transparent pieces are very appealing; they have a presence in a room yet don't seem to take up any space. The relationship between light and transparent materials is the key. Perspex in particular can play amazing visual tricks."

The BoBo design team in Brighton have also been working with Perspex to create lighting, although they have opted for a coloured, translucent finish. Glo-nuts, designed by Nick Gant and Tanya Dean, offer a multi-functional lighting concept, with sumptuous doughnut-shaped illuminated forms that can be stacked on the floor or mounted on the wall. Glo-nuts are manufactured from 5-mm (1/4 -in) Perspex Frost in a variety of fashionable colours and can be used for illumination or seating. Pillow is a new sculptural lighting panel with an amazingly soft visual and tactile quality. It is translucent and can be used to emit a range of different types of light.

Nick Avino, Perspex business manager says, "The new Frost colours were developed to meet the needs of today's designers who seek a fresh, inspired, and contemporary look. Colour and light are a medium in which designers such as BoBo can express their creativity." Colours available in the Frost range include Lemon Sorbet, a fresh yellow, Blush, a warm pink, and Aurora, a vibrant violet, as well as Polar White, Arctic Blue, Glacier Green, and Crystal Clear.

Sandblasted, coloured, or transparent acrylic sheet can be used to create dividing walls in the bathroom, either to break the room up into different zones (bath, toilet, basin), or to separate the bathroom from the rest of the living space while maximizing the flow of light.

As acrylic is more susceptible to scratching than glass, it is not best suited for areas of heavy wear such as the basin or bath. It can, however, be used extremely effectively for more decorative areas of the bathroom, such as back-lit light panels, bath panels, and shower screens.

Sanitary ware manufacturer Sottini has introduced acrylic sheet into the design of its latest bathroom suite. By marrying traditional ceramic with contemporary acrylic, Sottini's Philosophy suite combines the best of both worlds. The suite has a hardwearing and easy-to-clean ceramic surface area above a highly decorative base. The toilet base, basin pedestal, and the sides of the bath are wrapped in translucent frosted acrylic fitted with an LED light source. The Philosophy suite looks white until the light is turned on, when it takes on a subtle glow. The colour of the acrylic depends on the colour of the light used, so the bathroom can change from ice blue to sunny yellow, or even red, depending on your mood.

The Italian company Agape has a worldwide reputation for minimal, functional designs and its Chiocciola spiral shower is no exception. This translucent, sensuous piece would be the centrepiece of any design-conscious bathroom, and its free-standing fitting is as practical as it is decorative. A single sheet of pearly acrylic curls round itself to create a stand-alone shower enclosure set on a resin and quartz-composite shower tray. The chrome shower is fitted to the inside wall of the enclosure, finishing with a generous showerhead. The bather is enclosed in a crisp white space flooded with light, while the curving shape of the acrylic contains water splashes. Providing the correct plumbing is available, this stylish enclosure could sit as happily in the corner of a bedroom as it would in a bathroom. The shower becomes a self-contained pod as, once you have entered it, you are fully hidden from view.

above Change your bathroom to suit your mood. The Philosophy suite from Sottini changes colour according to the light bulb fitted behind the white acrylic panels. For real atmosphere, the overhead light can be switched off and the suite will glow in the dark.

right Spiralling round like a giant conch shell, Chiocciola from Agape is a self-contained shower enclosure in white acrylic with an integral showerhead.

left It looks like a crumpled piece of paper, but this imaginative lampshade is made out of a square of acrylic that has been printed with a pattern resembling creased and folded paper.

right Italian designer Jacopo Foggini extrudes brightly coloured plastic to make the sculptural shapes for his furniture and lighting.

right When acrylic is still in its liquid form, other elements can be added to it. The solid legs of this table incorporate strips of brightly coloured plastic, which add interest to an otherwise transparent piece.

Acrylic is not used to replace only glass; it is frequently used in place of materials such as china, wood, and even metal to make everyday household objects and decorative accessories. Occasional tables, lampshades, and lamp bases are used in living rooms; acrylic cutlery, jugs, and salad bowls have appeared in kitchens; and in bathrooms containers for toothbrushes and small storage units look fun and don't smash if dropped. Because acrylic is lightweight yet tough, and because it can be cut and heat-formed or moulded, its possibilities have captured the imagination of designers world-wide, and it is being used to replace traditional materials with great success.

Cutlery, for instance, has been reinterpreted by today's designers. We tend to think of cutlery as metal: whether stainless steel or silver, cutlery has a solid, enduring image. Plastic cutlery is functional, disposable; it isn't expected to last, and therefore the quality of its design isn't crucial. American designer Ralph Kramer has abandoned these preconceptions and designed a range of elegant plastic flatware for Mono Tabletop. Kramer's Filio flatware is dishwasher safe and available in four colours. The transparent design is both appealing and functional, and is a very real alternative to traditional metal.

Because acrylic is so hardwearing and is available in such a wide range of colours, it is particularly appealing for use in everyday household items, which serve a practical purpose while glowing in jewel-bright shades. Moss, in New York, for instance, includes in its household range a vacuum jug, designed by Lovegrove and Brown, which has an emerald acrylic casing around the glass liner.

Plastic may not be as expensive or be considered as prestigious as glass or ceramic, but it has come a long way from its purely functional roots. As more designers experiment with plastic — colouring it, cutting it, bending it, and stretching it — we will become more and more aware of just how beautiful this material can be. Acrylic bowls and vases may not be as fragile as glass, or as classic as ceramic, but the material has matured thanks to the imaginative input of designers worldwide, and should now be judged on its own merits, rather than as a cheap alternative to more traditional materials.

above Polycarbonate is a strong, rigid plastic that can be used to make furniture. The La Marie range of chairs from Kartell comes in a rainbow palette of colours, from red and orange to lilac, as well as clear.

right Coloured polycarbonate slats have been mounted horizontally on the wall and then lit from behind with bright strip lighting to brighten the walls of this otherwise industrial setting.

Polycarbonate is another widely used plastic, although it is not as popular as acrylic for domestic and contract interiors. Polycabonate is a strong, rigid thermoplastic, transparent or translucent, and is most commonly used in the manufacture of safety helmets, protective windows, and drinks bottles. Polycarbonate sheet can be used for interior design, although it is best suited to dividing walls and screens, as it is not strong enough to bear loads and can split. The interior design practice Forster Inc. used transparent polycarbonate sheet in a London office refurbishment. The company wanted to create as much light and space as possible within the building, and so the solid walls between the reception area, corridor, and meeting space were replaced with ribbed, double-skinned poycarbonate sheets set in a steel frame. Designer Jonathan Forster explains, "The twin panels gave an opaque effect so that you are aware of people behind the walls but you can't see what they are doing; there is privacy but you are not all cooped up."

To add an extra dimension, the ribbing runs horizontally on one panel and vertically on the other, and the two are lit internally to create a prismatic effect. Forster says, "Installing polycarbonate walls has allowed us to really open up the feel of the office and create a dialogue between spaces. It allowed a good mix of natural and artificial light. This was a low-budget project but we would have chosen polycarbonate anyway; it's easy to install, lightweight, fire retardant, and it creates a nice DIY touch."

Pigment can be added to polycarbonate to create coloured translucent sheets, and because thin polycarbonate sheets are pliable, they can be wrapped into tubular or conical shapes while remaining rigid. These properties have been employed by a number of lighting designers.

Lampholder 2000's Sailbuoy lights feature a tube of matt-finish polycarbonate in subtle shades of tangerine, lilac, and lemon. Lighting designer Martin Dannell has created conical polycarbonate lampshades in vibrant red and green.

The possibilities of polycarbonate have not been lost on furniture designers either: Italian company Kartell has been using it in its La Marie

left These decorative panels slide across the window to shield the shower from the window. As well as providing privacy, this is a practical solution, as the plastic is unaffected by splashes from the overhead shower.

chairs, made from a single sheet of transparent polycarbonate in glossy orange, red, and mauve.

As polycarbonate is a particularly rigid plastic, it is ideally suited to creating lightweight panels. If the thickness of the panel is correctly calculated in relation to its size, the polycarbonate should not bow or crumple but will keep its shape without the need for a supporting wood or metal frame. Because of this, sliding polycarbonate panels can be used instead of hinged doors on cabinets, or as an alternative to shutters at the window.

Sliding polycarbonate window screens are ideally suited to the bathroom, especially where a high degree of privacy is required. White polycarbonate allows plenty of light into the room but will completely screen those inside from the outside world. It is more practical than curtains because it is impervious to water and steam and can be wiped clean. Polycarbonate is also the right choice if the window does not need to be permanently translucent. The panels easily slide away from the window when the bathroom is not in use, so that the view can again be enjoyed. As with acrylic, polycarbonate can be screen-printed to create a patterned surface, introducing colour to the room while still retaining translucency.

Clear, ridged polycarbonate sheet is also suitable as a simple roofing material for sheds, garages, or verandas. The clarity of the material allows natural light into areas that might otherwise have no windows, which is vital for the gardener who may be growing seedlings or over-wintering plants in the shed. If the panels are set at an angle with one side slightly raised, the ridges will carry away any rain, and as the panels are so lightweight they are extremely easy for the amateur to lift and fit into place.

Ridged polycarbonate sheets, readily available from DIY stores, have in the past had a rather utilitarian image. However, if fitted properly and neatly finished off they can look good, especially when used in a contemporary setting where other plastics have already been used. It is certainly worth considering this method of lightweight practical roofing for a veranda or covered walkway where only a limited degree of shelter is required, particularly if the project is being kept to a tight budget.

above A redundant fireplace is given a new lease of life. A table lamp is set in the cavity and then masked by a frosted polycarbonate panel. The panel softens the glare of the lamp to a gentle glow.

While acrylic and polycarbonate are both rigid plastics, PVC is another widely used plastic valued for its soft, rather than stiff, quality.

Polyvinyl chloride, known as PVC or vinyl, is a thermoplastic formed by the polymerization of vinyl chloride. It is resistant to fire, chemicals, and moisture and is easily dyed. PVC can be softened by mixing it with a plasticizer, which prevents it from becoming rigid, and it is this quality above all that has contributed to its popularity. In the 1950s vinyl found a special place in the hearts of Americans as an upholstery material that would last for years in the average family home. Rigid PVC is used for pipes and other moulded products, while the flexible version is commonly used for food packaging and clothing.

PVC has a highly tactile quality, which is why it is increasingly used for clothing other than practical waterproof coats, such as high-fashion trousers and dresses. Anyone who saw Michelle Pfeiffer in her skintight black PVC Catwoman outfit in Tim Burton's 1992 film *Batman Returns* will understand the sex appeal of PVC. This appeal has been translated to furniture by London company Ennemlaghi, with its gorgeously exotic red PVC armchair, and by the Italian company Edra, in the form of the invitingly feminine Anemone chair.

PVC has also been used successfully to create a few design paradoxes. Household items that we normally think of as being rigid, such as basins, tablemats and lampshades, can be manufactured out of thick sheets of flexible PVC. Agape has created a fine example in its bendy yet practical Foglio basins, which are guaranteed to surprise. And, because of its resistance to heat, PVC can also be used for tablemats, table cloths, and coasters.

As with so many plastics, PVC is increasingly used in the design-conscious interior, where its tactile nature can be fully appreciated. PVC readily accepts dye, so that transparent and translucent lengths can be produced in anything from pretty pastels to shocking pink or even black. The combination of colour, flexibility, and transparency has proved irresistible to some of today's key designers, as we shall see over the next few pages.

above Because of its pliable nature, PVC drapes and folds much like cloth. A transparent PVC curtain can be used as a room divider that pulls out of the way when not in use.

left Portable, comfortable, and ultimately disposable, this pair of inflated armchairs is a humorous take on the traditional fireside chair.

One of the most eye-catching furniture designs to appear in the last couple of years is the Cube Chair from design team Ennemlaghi. The iMac allowed us to see the internal workings of our computer, and was followed closely by Artemide's e.light. Ennemlaghi has now exposed the interior of the armchair. The Cube Chair is constructed from 224 springs of various densities, assembled by hand and covered in a soft, transparent PVC skin, saddle-stitched together. The method for making the chair is traditional; the result is anything but. The chair is so eye-catching that the first model is currently on display at the Museum of Modern Art in New York.

The Cube Chair, which is available in clear, red, or mauve PVC, is fascinating because you can see through it; it's a chair but it's more than a simple piece of furniture; and it's in racy colours. For extra interest, the chair can be lit internally, so that the full complexity of the internal spring system can be seen. This effect is particularly suited to the red PVC chair, which appears to radiate warmth when lit from beneath. The chair is ideal for contract use, as PVC is fire resistant, wipe-clean, and comfortable.

In complete contrast to the Cube Chair's structured square shape, Anemone, from Edra's 2001 collection, is a soft, voluptuous seat. Designed by Fernando and Umberto Campana, Anemone features lengths of soft, pink PVC tubing woven over an oval metal frame to create a loosely textured organic shape. The tubing is fixed in place to provide support in the centre of the chair while the remaining lengths trail down to the floor.

They may look completely different, but the Cube and Anemone chairs both combine the soft, tactile nature of PVC with colour and transparency. These are not rigid pieces of furniture, but comfortable, welcoming chairs which, although highly visual, have been designed to serve a purpose. The structure of the chair looks so loose, you imagine that if you sat in it you would fall straight through to the floor. In reality, although the PVC is flexible enough to hug your shape, it fully supports your weight and springs back into shape when not in use.

above For a witty update on the classic armchair, Ennemlaghi used a traditional spring and frame system for its Cube Chair, but upholstered it in red PVC so that the internal support becomes part of the overall design.

right PVC has a soft, almost drapable, quality, making it a sympathetic material for relaxed seating. The Anemone chair from Edra provides soft, supple support with a web of pink PVC tubing.

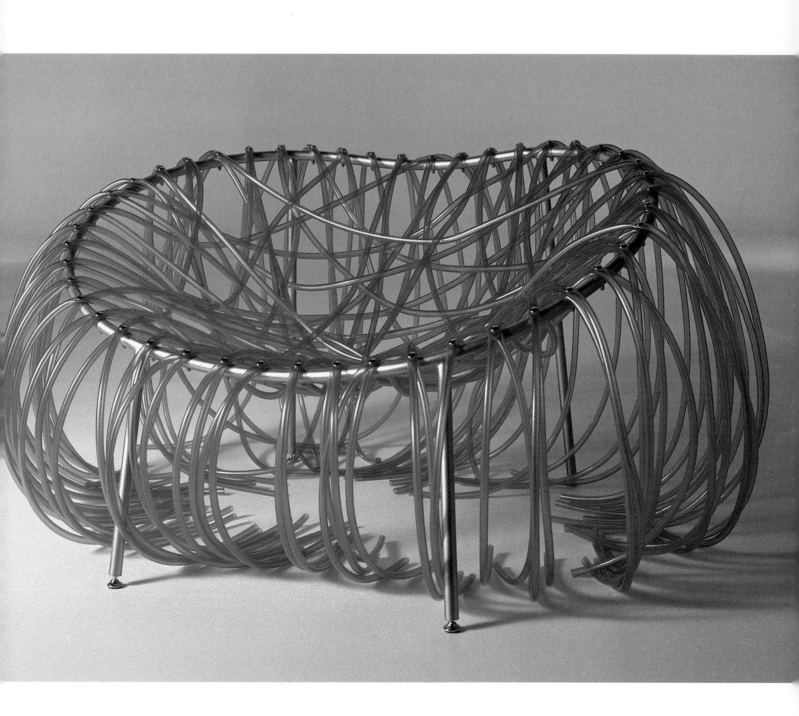

left Stella Corrall works in PVC to create domestic accessories, such as these tablemats and coasters, as well as wall hangings and lampshades. She bonds lengths of coloured and clear PVC together to create a striped PVC sheet.

right The PVC curtain in this kitchen is made up of a patchwork of red, white, orange, and yellow squares that, because of their transparency, create an effect similar to that of a stained glass window.

Despite its soft, pliable nature PVC is surprisingly heat resistant, making it suitable for use in lighting. It retains colour extremely well and is not prone to fading when exposed to natural or artificial light. Manchester designer Stella Corrall has harnessed these properties for her range of coloured PVC lampshades. Stella has been working with plasticized PVC for a number of years. She hand-dyes batches of PVC and creates designs by cutting strips of the coloured material, which are bonded back together in stripes or mosaic patterns. This is a labour-intensive process but worth it, as the resulting sheets of PVC have all the subtle depth and colour variation of woven cloth. Corrall's PVC remains translucent, so that light shines through the multicoloured PVC with an almost stained-glass effect. Corrall prefers to work in single colour groups, with stripes ranging from, say, pink to red, or alternate dark blue and light blue interspersed with transparent sections.

The textile quality of Corrall's PVC need not be limited to lighting. She has designed large-scale wall hangings and flooring for various interior-design projects, and on a much smaller scale, she cuts sheets of her striped PVC into 10cm (4in) squares to make heat-resistant coasters.

In the bathroom, PVC can be used for shower curtains, where its soft draping quality allows it to hang in gentle coloured or transparent folds. More surprisingly, PVC can also be used for basins, as demonstrated by Italian bathroom specialists Agape. Designed by Giampaolo Benedini, the innovative Foglio basin is made from a flexible sheet of PVC, which sits on a curved tubular support. In subtle shades of orange, yellow, grey, and violet, Foglio is designed to make a real impact in the bathroom, with the transparent flexible "bowl" providing a striking contrast to the standard ceramic basin. The PVC section can even be replaced, so the basin can be updated to match the décor. Although the basin dips slightly towards the central plughole, Foglio is a noticeably shallow design. Agape says it researched the way washbasins are used today and found that the "water-containing" function is virtually unused. This wide yet shallow design is therefore perfectly suited to the contemporary bathroom, as it simply collects the water from a running tap.

For designers looking for a slightly more substantial plastic, polypropylene is a white translucent thermoplastic formed by the polymerization of propene. It is tough and resistant to water, solvents, and high temperatures. It is made into fibres that can be used in rope, is produced as thin rolls of film, is used in making carrier bags, and can be moulded into shapes.

Although often used in its natural white state, polypropylene can be dyed any colour. It has a crisp rigidity, making it suitable for the production of furniture and fittings that require a more solid result.

The Anglo-Swiss design partnership black+blum has used polypropylene in the production of some of its lights. Daniel Black and Martin Blum joined forces in 1998, after meeting at the University of Northumbria while studying design. They started working as a design consultancy, which evolved over the years into a company producing its own collection of lively lighting solutions. The philosophy of the company is to show that "designed" products can be made affordable without compromising their quality. The aim of black+blum is to create innovative products that will charm and entertain.

The company's work is characterized by a quirky sense of humour, giving their range of lights individual personalities. Bag of Light, for instance, is a collection of brightly coloured polypropylene lights, carefully bent and folded to look like red, yellow, and purple carrier bags. Little Devil is another eye-catching tabletop design in bright red, which projects an image of an angel on to the surface behind it, while its forked tail trails on the floor.

Polypropylene is perfectly suited to these designs, because it has a dense yet paper-like quality that makes it more translucent than plastics such as acrylic or polycarbonate. Light shines through the material but the source of the light is completely obscured, so that the shape of the piece rather than the light it emits becomes the main focus.

The company black+blum is now planning to expand its product portfolio into a houseware collection, again featuring designs in plastic, to maintain the company's ethos of high design at an affordable price.

left Moulded polypropylene cubes stack one on top of the other for a neat display column. Although polypropylene has a dense appearance, natural light can still penetrate it.

right black+blum's Bag of Light can sit on the table or on the floor. It looks good on its own or in a group of several contrasting colours. The rigid quality of polypropylene creates the sharp folds in the "bag".

Because polypropylene is white in its natural state it does not on first appearance seem to have any translucent qualities. Furniture made out of this plastic has none of the light, transient appeal of that produced in transparent glass or acrylic. However, if a bulb is fitted within the piece, its light shows through, instantly bringing the furniture to life – polypropylene is almost, but not quite, opaque, and obviously the thinner it is the better its translucency.

Several furniture designers have produced pieces in polypropylene, marrying its seemingly dense appearance with a hidden light source. Probably the most quirky of these is the Tooth, from Thai design group Propaganda. The group aims to bring a "humorous approach to the way we live with life, turning everyday objects into fun yet functional works of art". Tooth is a white polypropylene stool shaped like a molar that when lit radiates a gentle glow. You can sit on it, use it as an occasional table or just enjoy it as it is.

Designer Kazuhiro Yamanaka focuses on "forcing maximum impact with minimum use of material"; a policy embodied in his How Slow the Wind illuminated chair. The swivel chair is made out of a simple sheet of white polypropylene with a slit cut into it. Into this slit is inserted a drum on a rotating turntable. The plastic sheet forms the arm and back of the chair, while a fluorescent light is fitted inside the seat. This elegant design looks fragile but is surprisingly comfortable to sit in.

Aimed more at the bar and night-club market, boo!, from Totem Design, is an interactive polypropylene seat with a suede cushion. Born of Newton's second law that "every action has an equal and opposite reaction", boo!, and the larger bootoo, are multifunctional sensory furniture – sit and boo! automatically lights up; stand and it's off; turn boo! on, remove it's cushion and you have a table, a light, or even a dance podium. The fully sealed, moulded, circular polypropylene base houses a low-energy light fitting that can be wired into the floor or battery-powered, and both boo! and bootoo are available in a choice of five colours, including light blue, pink, and lime.

above Sit on the boo! stool from Totem Design and it automatically lights up, stand and it turns off. Made from translucent polypropylene, boo! can be a stool, a table, or a dance podium.

left The illuminated chair from Kazuhiro Yamanaka utilizes the light-diffusing properties of polypropylene for the drum-shaped seat and the plastic's natural rigidity for the chair back.

above Soft, pliable silicone may be associated most readily with breast implants, but it also makes great light fittings. The Bubble light from Mathmos is a perfect sphere of coloured silicone containing a rechargeable light.

Silicone is a synthetic polymer consisting of chains of alternating silicon and oxygen atoms. It is perhaps most commonly known as the synthetic material used in breast implants, so it may come as a surprise that it has also been used for contemporary lighting. Silicone plastics are resistant to heat and water and do not conduct electricity.

Silicone plastic is a clouded translucent material that is pleasingly soft to the touch. Because it does not conduct electricity it can safely be used to contain a power source. Mathmos, the company that launched the first lava lamp in 1963 (a design created by Craven Walker and based on a wartime egg timer), has long had a reputation for producing fun, imaginative lighting concepts.

The company's Bubble lights, designed by Aaron Rincover, are tactile silicone spheres in a choice of red, green, or blue. Measuring 8cm (3¼ in) in diameter, the spheres glow with a rechargeable light. Bubble lights will stay alight for up to five hours and are as easily recharged as a mobile phone, so they are totally portable. They have a splashproof seal so they can be used inside and out. In addition to their novelty value, Bubble lights can be extremely decorative, especially if used *en masse*. They can be used instead of candles, strategically placed around a room to create an ambient atmosphere, or piled high in a fruit bowl to make a modern table centrepiece.

In 2001 Mathmos also introduced Bubble Nest, an aluminium cup with a power lead in which Bubble lights can be contained and recharged when not in use. The Nest also allows you to hang Bubble on the wall or place it on a surface without fear of it rolling off. Bubble can be illuminated while in the Nest, creating a pool of coloured light that reflects back from the metal surface.

Silicone has a unique texture, and holds its shape while gently giving to surface pressure. Like beanbags or juggling balls, a silicone sphere is extremely pleasing to hold, and with the added interest of an integral light source, the Bubble lights become irresistible to pick up and hold. Scattered around the house or garden these lights will definitely attract attention.

right The Lucci-Co coffee tables and Lucci-Waa wall tiles are by Abbi Kiki, who works with a variety of new and recycled plastics to create illuminated furniture.

In the natural world, resin is used to describe the sticky, translucent substance produced by trees, in particular conifers. This sounds rather unappealing, but the gluey substance results in amber, the beautiful transparent yellow or reddish material that can be carved and polished to make jewellery. Admittedly, amber is the result of fossilization and takes millions of years to produce, but the results are mouthwatering.

In the modern world we don't have to wait so long. Synthetic resin can be produced from manufactured polymers, resulting in a viscous liquid that, when set, becomes a solid, transparent material. This can then be coloured and polished to create the same appealing characteristics as its natural counterpart.

Italian design company Alessi has produced many simple but desirable objects in resin over the years, and its Big Bubbles soap dishes certainly boast a "must have" appeal. Designed for Alessi by Stafano Giovannoni, the lozenge-shaped soap dishes look like giant transparent boiled sweets. The design is enhanced by the choice of four mouth-watering colours — lime, lemon, blue, and violet — and the simple word SOAP stamped into the base.

Alessi was founded in 1921, in the little village of Omegna in the foothills of the Alps, and now supplies stylish domestic accessories to homes all over the world. The company says its success lies in "our ability to reconcile typical industrial needs with our tendency, both intellectual and spiritual, to consider ourselves more as a research laboratory in the field of applied arts."

Because resin starts in a liquid form, other elements can be incorporated into it before it sets hard. Items such as paperweights made out of transparent resin can be moulded into a spherical shape, while holding at their heart the fragile head of a dandelion flower or a single softly curling feather.

One area where the use of moulded resin has come to the fore is in decorative or humorous toilet seats. A seaside theme in the bathroom can be continued with the addition of a resin toilet seat filled with shells.

above This appealing little three-legged table has been made by pouring liquid resin into a mould. The result is a piece of furniture made out of one solid yet transparent lump of resin.

right The cast-resin body of the Mary Jane console table by David Khouri partially obscures the objects within, so that their vague shapes and frosted colours become part of the overall design.

left Knoll has set fabric in high-performance resin to create the Imago range of decorative sheets. The rigid sheets are used here to create translucent screens that divide one end of the room into individual work spaces.

right This reception desk is clad in Knoll's Imago resin sheets. A ring of the same material is suspended above the desk, making it the focal point of the lobby.

Just as amber appears to glow when light passes through it, so coloured synthetic resin has the same magical appearance. This quality can still be seen when the material is set against a solid background and used in tiles.

The Natural Tile Company has a reputation for using alternative materials for tiles, with ranges made out of glass or metal as well as the more conventional ceramic. The company also produce the Active range of resin tiles. Liquid acrylic resin is coloured and set in tile moulds. They are then machine-finished to give a smooth surface, and backed with silver leaf to enhance the tiles' light-reflective quality. Available in three shades of blue, three shades of green, and three shades of orange, the tiles are both water- and heat-resistant, and suitable for use in the bathroom or kitchen. Like natural resin, the tiles, particularly those in the orange colourways, are extremely appealing to the eye and to the touch. They lift what would otherwise be a flat, tiled surface into a visual and tactile treat. Resin was chosen as the most suitable material for the Active tiles, as a particularly chunky result was desired, which would have been both heavy and expensive in glass. The tiles also have a slightly frosted finish that becomes translucent when wet and returns to the frosted finish when dry, hence the name Active. For maximum effect, the tiles require complementary lighting to bring the translucency of the resin alive.

Resin can also be used to encapsulate materials for use in screens and shelving. US company Knoll produces the Imago range of decorative sheets, designed by Susan Tick, which encapsulate fabric in high-performance resin. This new, hard-surfaced material provides designers with an option that combines the best qualities of fabric, resin, and glass. Tick has used a variety of fabrics within her range, so that Imago sheets are available in a choice of bright colours, metallics, and minimal sheers. Imago can be sawn, drilled, punched, riveted, bolted, hot-stamped, die-cut, and thermoformed. It is shatterproof, resistant to scratches and fingerprints, and is suitable for myriad applications, from panels and screens to furniture, window treatments, and shelving. Imago sheeting is sold in 1,200- x 2,400-mm (4- x 8-ft) sheets, and is half the weight of glass.

fabric and paper

"Western paper turns away the light while our paper seems to take it in, to envelop it gently like the soft surface of first snowfall."   Junchiro Tanizaki   Translucent fabric and paper add an ethereal dimension to the interior, providing a softer complement to the more rigid elements within the scheme, while gently filtering harsh light.

left Lengths of sheer fabric will add a romantic dimension to a room, whether draped at the window, where they move gently in the breeze, or hung from the ceiling to create a simple room divider.

In the quest to maximize the flow of natural light into our homes and workplaces, the transparent interior runs the risk of being stark. Large expanses of glass and plastics will appear crisp and clean to some, but to others this transparent theme will appear cold, even harsh. It is possible, however, to soften the look without losing the light.

Sheer fabrics, from intricate net curtains to simple voile panels, provide the answer. Sheer fabrics bring a sense of movement to the room; the slightest breeze or draught and they gently undulate, blurring the hard lines between window frame and wall. Full-length white sheer curtains fitted at the window or over glass doors and walls will also filter very bright sunlight, resulting in a more softly lit interior.

Lengths of fabric can be used imaginatively to personalize a room. Complicated swags and drapes will contribute to a more romantic, feminine theme, while a flat fabric panel, either hung from a pole or simply nailed to the window frame, is perfectly suited to the minimalist interior.

Sheer fabrics are also extremely useful in the light versus privacy argument. Few of us live in such remote locations that we can afford to keep our windows completely open to the outside world. In most homes the bathroom and bedroom windows in particular need some form of screening. A lightweight fabric at the window is a pretty alternative to heavy curtains, roller blinds or even textured window panes that, although practical during the day, can appear featureless and black at night.

However, fabric need not be restricted to curtains. Stretched over a wooden frame, translucent fabric makes the perfect folding screen or room divider. A fabric panel hung in a doorway replaces a solid door, while subtly highlighting the transition from one room to another.

Fabric can also be a useful way of introducing splashes of colour into a decorating scheme; even gossamer-fine sheers can still be colourful. Bright sari-red or orange silk-organza hung at the window will glow with colour during the day and provide an exotic backdrop in the evenings. Pastel sheers in pistachio green or palest yellow bring a sense of spring to an otherwise white room.

To add greater interest in terms of texture and surface decoration, sheer fabrics can be embroidered, either with a contrasting colour or with the same colour thread to create a tone on tone design. A number of designers are working with appliqué techniques, often using leaf and flower shapes cut from felt or velvet, which are sown on to the body fabric. More unusual additions include real materials, such as light-weight shells or feathers.

There is a wide range of sheer fabrics available, from synthetic polyester to natural silk. Each fabric will have a slightly different feel and body, making it more or less suitable for specific applications. Before buying fabric, check its individual properties. Unroll a good length to see how sheer it is and its exact colour; the colour will always look much deeper when the fabric is folded or on the roll. If you want a filmy, draping fabric, a fine cotton voile will give a soft billowing effect, whereas an organza or organdie sheer has more body and will present a stiff, less ethereal, result. In contract rather than domestic locations, flame retardancy will be a major consideration, so here the high-performance synthetic sheers, such as polyester, are a good choice.

There is also a whole array of specialist fabrics to choose from, including laser-cut panels that resemble Japanese paper cuts, lustrous metallics, and contemporary open-weave textural panels.

Fabric can be stitched into swags and pleats, knotted and draped over a curtain pole, or simply nailed or pinned to the wall to create stylish results. A single length of fabric will have a pretty, simple appeal, while the more fabric used the more romantic and opulent the scheme can appear. Trims and fittings also have an impact on the final result. Wooden curtain poles appear more rustic, while sleek chrome adds an urban touch. A length of sheer fabric can be left completely unadorned, but the addition of a decorative fringe or appliquéd pattern will make it more of a feature. The possibilities really are endless. For instance, too-long curtains that trail and pool onto the floor, or exaggerated treatments where lengths are wrapped loosely around the curtain pole, will look dramatic.

above Text printed on to plain sheer fabric lifts it out of the ordinary without introducing any colours that might compete with the décor.

left Tiny felt leaves have been stitched on to this fabric to create little spots of colour on an otherwise completely sheer background. Hung against a vibrantly painted wall, the fabric serves to soften the colour while adding texture.

Net curtains do not have a good reputation, and are more likely to evoke images of endless rows of safe suburban houses than stylish interiors. Bright white nylon nets may serve a useful purpose, protecting the household from the prying eyes of nosy neighbours, but they are hardly at the cutting edge of design. However, all this could be about to change with a new generation of net for curtains set to take this historically bland furnishing fabric distinctly up market.

The term net applies to any open-mesh fabric; it is usually white and manufactured from nylon or cotton. Traditionally, net for curtains has featured detailed flower and leaf patterns interspersed with more open-work netting. The new nets have dispensed with the flowers and feature instead bold geometric designs, spots, and even script. These are crisp, contemporary fabrics designed to provide a degree of privacy while creating a highly decorative effect at the window. If net can shrug off its *passé* image, these new nets should be able to leave the suburbs behind and move right into the heart of the city.

Some of the top names in furnishing fabrics have brought out contemporary nets, including Sahco Hesslein, Brunschwig & Fils, and Edmund Petit. Sahco Hesslein's Euforia design is an extremely fine net underlined with a larger squared design, a geometric pattern that bears little resemblance to the traditional floral net curtain. In contrast, Brunschwig & Fils has adopted a humorous approach to net curtains with an all-over spot pattern, showing how the fine net background of the cloth can be used to carry a motif without losing its overall translucent quality. This thought is carried further by Velum Villeprint from Edmund Petit, which incorporates finely embroidered letters of the alphabet, randomly scattered over the net background.

Alternatively, if even the slightest decorative detail is too much there is plenty of completely plain net available. This allows for a window treatment that gives a degree of privacy, without becoming a style statement that might clash with other furnishings. Because of its open weave, net does not create soft drapes but it will hold its shape and carry pleats and folds well.

left A tree pattern embroidered on a sheer fabric brings this translucent panel to life.

right Long lengths of arctic white cotton trail elegantly onto the floor of this living room.

left A fine weave with an integral, textural pattern filters light and blurs shapes.

left A selection of natural fabrics such as cotton and linen have been stretched over frames to create a suspended sculpture full of movement. The choice of natural colours and simple circular shapes gives this installation an organic appeal.

above Lengths of fabric stretched between pillars have been used partially to screen the large windows in this dining area. The panels are an interesting alternative to blinds or curtains, and provide privacy while maintaining the levels of natural light.

Natural fibres such as silk, wool, linen, and cotton have been used in textile design for hundreds of years, and still feature in a significant proportion of the fabrics available today. After a slight dip in popularity during the 1960s and 1970s, when newly discovered synthetic alternatives such as nylon and rayon became all the rage, natural fibres have enjoyed a revival in more recent years. The popularity of the natural look has resulted in extensive sales of unbleached cotton and natural linen, with their muted, off-white tones contributing significantly to the neutral, minimalist interior. Natural fibres also have a higher perceived value than their synthetic counterparts, and are often coveted for this reason alone. Silk, cotton, and even linen and wool can be used to make translucent cloth, either by using very fine threads to make sheer voile, or in an open-weave or cut cloth that lets light through.

Voile is a lightweight fabric, plain-woven with an open texture, made from hard, twisted yarns that give it a crisper feeling than the similarly woven, although softer, muslin. Cotton is ideally suited to the production of muslin and voile as it can be spun into extremely fine threads. Cotton from Egypt and the West Indies is usually of superior quality to that from the USA and Asia, because of the initial length of the staple fibres.

Silk is obtained by unwinding the filament surrounding the cocoons formed by silk worms. This luxury fibre is surprisingly strong and naturally lustrous. Silk takes vibrant colours well, and these are further enhanced by its natural sheen. Extremely fine silk cloth is translucent, and creates an almost stained-glass effect when hung at a window.

Linen and wool do not seem suited for use in translucent fabrics, as both are more substantial, heavy-duty fibres. However, opaque linen cloth can be cut to make a design incorporating peep-holes that let light through and offer a tantalizing glimpse of what lies beyond. Cut linen is suitable for roller blinds and room dividers and, in its natural state, has the same colour and textural appearance as parchment. Wool is used in loose, open weaves that can be wrapped around glass light fittings or used as window hangings. The woolly, frayed ends of the yarn provide the cloth with a textural quality.

Rayon was first developed in 1891 in Paris by Louis Marie Hilaire Bernigaut, the Count of Chardonnet. He was searching for a way to produce man-made silk and had noticed, from studying silk worms, how they produced a liquid that hardened on exposure to the air. But it was not until the 1920s, and the discovery of nylon, that cloth made from synthetic fibres really took off. There is now a dazzling array of synthetic fabrics available, which are far more durable and far less flammable than their ancestors.

Polyester has been the most influential synthetic in textile design. It is a man-made resin made from alcohols and acids, which is used to make artificial fibres that are then woven into cloth. It is flame-retardant, durable, and resistant to creasing. Polyester cloth is lighter in weight than natural materials and has a much lower water-retention capacity, resulting in greater breathability and faster drying. Polyester also tends to "pill" less than natural fibres and is less susceptible to fading, as it has a natural resistance to UV light. Polyester fibre can be used on its own or in blends with natural fibres such as cotton.

Trevira is one of the leading manufacturers of polyester thread for both interiors and clothing. Trevira has recently produced a monofilament polyester fibre that produces a cloth with the high transparency and gossamer lightness of organza, but with good drape characteristic. Combining monofilament with other yarns produces fabrics ranging from semi-transparent to opaque. Monofilament fibres have greater sheen and surface reflection than other polyester fibres, and high flex resistance, so that the cloth feels soft. If a crinkle effect is required, the fibre can be fixed with a heat treatment in a way that is both stable and wash-resistant.

UK company Skopos has produced a range of delicate transparent fabrics using polyester filaments. The fabrics are designed to diffuse light, giving rooms a soft feel. The voiles and sheers are all produced in 100 per cent polyester and are inherently flame-retardant. Fabrics are plain or available in striped or blocked patterns and are aimed at the demanding contract market, where fabrics are expected to look good as well as being easy to clean and able to withstand the rigours of hotel life.

above Alternate transparent and translucent diamond shapes are edged with gold for this large-scale fabric design, which contributes to the opulent setting.

right Man-made fibres have come a long way since the invention of rayon in 1891. Contemporary synthetic fabrics are lightweight and are far more pleasing to the touch then their predecessors, as well as being durable and water-resistant.

left Sahco Hesslein has incorporated fine steel wire into the composition of its Sinus fabric. The result is a sheer cloth with a high surface sheen that is extremely hard-wearing.

right Natural stonewashed linen has been updated with a hi-tech treatment. Daylight from Studio Warwick is laser-cut to produce frayed holes that allow tantalizing glimpses of what lies beyond.

Voile fabrics are often chosen to be as unobtrusive as possible. They may soften the lines of the room and provide a degree of privacy, but the very word "sheer" implies that they have very little presence within the interior scheme – they are hardly there at all. However, there is a breed of hi-tech fabrics that, although translucent, have not been designed to fade gently into the background. These are bold, brash statement fabrics, not content with providing a backdrop but determined to dominate centre stage.

The inclusion of metal threads in fabric has led this trend for in-your-face designs. Sahco Hesslein in Germany, for example, has a sheer cloth launched in 2002 called simply Copper, which can be sculpted and holds its shape thanks to its 90 per cent metal content combined with just ten per cent polyester. Fine wire in fabric results in an enlivening sheen that catches and reflects back the light in a multitude of colours, lending the cloth an iridescent quality. Swedish company Kinnasand combines polyester with fine steel wire for its shimmering Sinus cloth, which has a silvery blue tint to it. Studio Warwick in London includes colourful metallic sheers in its Opulence collection, providing a striking contrast to its soft linen and cotton prints.

Research is continuing into creating new and exciting fabrics that not only use fibres in imaginative ways but also incorporate the latest technology. There are textiles that have included fibre optics woven into the cloth, so that the translucent cloth not only lets light in but also generates it, gently glowing in the dark. Different effects can be achieved by pleating and draping the fabric.

New technology has also opened up the door to more imaginative uses of opaque fabric. Laser-cutting has allowed designers to create unusual pieces from otherwise plain cloth, cutting random holes in densely woven cotton and linen for a frayed, punk look, or structured patterns to create a filigree effect. These cut fabrics can be so delicate in appearance, and so artistically executed, that using them purely as curtains would be a crime; they should be fully displayed as a screen, or perhaps hung on the wall as a futuristic equivalent to medieval tapestries.

The Jakob Schlaepfer collection for the Swiss company Création Baumann is quite simply stunning, combining great creativity with exceptional textile know-how. Transparency has been a key theme for Jakob Schlaepfer, with fabric that relies heavily on its interaction with light to reach its full visual impact.

The inspiration for Kirie came from Japanese paper cuts. Filigree, floral, and geometric motifs are cut into black cloth using a laser. The cloth, which looks like paper, is a fine polyester satin with a wax coating. The intricacy of the cut-work is extraordinary, with fragile leaves, petals, and stems suspended against a background of light.

Schlaepfer again used laser technology to produce the more contemporary Lola and Lela designs. Worked from softly draping polyester chiffon, Lola features an all-over pattern of dots cut through the already transparent chiffon. The sections cut from the cloth have not been removed, but remain barely attached, hanging suspended from the bottom of the cut circle. Lola's sister-design Lela has laser-cut appliqués sewn on to the ground cloth in contrasting colours.

According to Création Baumann, "Light is a topical subject and the Jakob Schlaepfer collection interprets this theme with much passion and lyricism." Materials that are usually the prerogative of high technology are transformed into enchanting and eye-catching fabrics.

Luminoso, another of Jakob Schlaepfer's designs, incorporates bundles of glass fibre-optics held between two layers of tulle. Fed from a light source, each glass fibre transports light to the interface, giving the appearance of hundreds of tiny stars. Lucciola is another hi-tech fabric, featuring free-hanging stems the ends of which have been adorned with butterflies and beetles, attached to the finest polyester monofilament. During the day the polyester foil of the appliqué work appears a delicate green; in the dark the true nature of the material emerges, shimmering brightly fluorescent.

left Lola is a softly draping polyester chiffon.
For added surface texture and transparency,
laser-cut dots are suspended from the surface.

left Lucciola comes alive at night, when the free-hanging stems, the ends of which have been adorned with butterflies and beetles, shimmer brightly fluorescent. During the day the polyester foil of the appliqué-work appears green.

below The base cloth for Kirie is black polyester satin coated in wax. Filigree floral motifs, inspired by Japanese paper cuts, have then been laser-cut into the fabric.

In ancient Egypt the pith from the flowering stems of the tall *Cyperus papyrus* plant, which grew along the banks of the Nile, was cut into strips that were soaked and pressed together into thin sheets. These were dried to form papyrus, a material for writing on favoured by the Egyptians, Greeks, and Romans.

Paper as we know it today was invented by the Chinese in the 2nd century. This early paper was hand-made in single sheets from processed fibres such as rags, and natural fibres from hemp and bark. Paper was introduced to medieval Europe by the Moors, eventually superseding parchment made from goat or sheep skin as the standard material for written and printed documents. The first machines to make continuous rolls (or webs) of paper were introduced in France in the late 18th century. From the 19th century, wood pulp and cellulose were the principal materials used in the manufacture of paper, while plant fibres and rags continued to be used to make high-quality papers.

Throughout the ages the main use of paper has been for books and documents, but the translucent quality of paper has not gone unrecognized, and this seemingly fragile material has been used for light fittings and screens (*see page 130*). Few houses in the 1970s were complete without large, spherical pendant lights made out of paper-covered wire frames, cheap and cheerful fittings that made a feature of a hanging light while softening the glare of the bulb. Contemporary paper light-fittings are available today, still based around the principle of a lightweight wooden or wire frame supporting a stretched paper skin.

Because paper is initially soft, contrasting materials, such as glass fibres, coloured cotton threads, or even dried flowers, can be added to the pulp before drying to create a more textured, ornamental effect. These decorative papers can be used in light panels, or even laminated between sheets of glass, to create translucent screens and walling. Paper is recyclable and biodegradable, so its use as a material for home furnishings — an alternative to less eco-friendly plastics — may well increase as we become more ecologically aware.

above Double doors in wood and paper create an art deco effect in this living room. The muted colour scheme and the carefully selected ornaments develop the theme.

left A long corridor has been panelled using thick paper stretched over wooden batons. The light behind the panelling highlights the fibrous texture of the paper.

From the middle of the third century, paper manufactured in China was imported into Japan as an extremely prized commodity. The Japanese recognized the value of this new material, not just for writing but for its decorative nature. As paper-making experts gradually settled in Japan, the country developed its own paper production in the 6th century. The trade grew rapidly with washi (Japanese handmade paper) primarily made out of native plants such as hemp and kozo. Washi is thin and refined, yet very strong, a result of adding a viscose liquid taken from the root of the hibiscus plant. With this additional strength, washi was used for clothing, oiled paper umbrellas, fans, and lacquered paper furniture, as well as the famous shoji screens.

Shoji not only serve the practical function of partitioning space and keeping out draughts; the diffused light also responds to the Japanese aesthetic sensitivity to the changing time of day and season. The delicate harmony between light and colour is often associated in western culture with stained glass. In Japan, shoji are enjoyed in a similar way in the homes of ordinary people, with the white purity of washi transmitting the spirit of nature from outside to inside.

Shoji screens are constructed from a wooden panel with the translucent paper fixed to one side. The screens can be static, or may incorporate sliding panels to allow access from one area to another. Traditional Japanese dwellings were timber-framed, with shoji panels used internally to create versatile spaces within the home. The beauty of shoji screens lies in their versatility: in the contemporary interior they can be used as room dividers, wardrobe doors, window treatments, or fixed or free-standing panels. The ancient concept looks contemporary and is increasingly relevant in open-plan living spaces. It is also practical, as damaged sections can easily be removed and replaced within the screen. Traditional paper is not always appropriate for shoji screens, but a similar effect can be achieved with lightweight translucent plastic such as polypropylene sheet. Shoji are quite simply the marriage of simplicity, functionality, and beauty.

above Despite their ancient history, shoji screens look perfectly at home in the modern interior. Because they slide open they are also space-efficient, as they do not swing out into the room.

right A contemporary Japanese-style home combines glass and shoji screens. When the weather allows, one side of this room can be opened to the garden completely by sliding the paper and wood screen to one side.

left Paper reacts well with light, softening the glare of the sun. White paper blinds can be lowered at midday, creating a more temperate atmosphere indoors.

right A fine rattan weave has been used to create the rounded shapes for these floor lamps. The rattan is then coated in damp squares of translucent paper that, when dry, form a taut skin over the frame.

Most of us have at some point, probably during early childhood, enjoyed the delights of creating a shape using papier-mâché. This is the art of sticking small squares of paper soaked in glue on to a mould. Once the papier-mâché has dried hard, the mould is removed and the resulting shape can be decorated and varnished for extra durability. This basic principle, although more stylishly executed than the misshapen creations of our youth, can be applied to the creation of paper light fittings. By soaking small squares of translucent paper in glue, you can build up a shape on a frame of wood or metal to create a rigid yet charmingly fragile-looking lampshade.

Paper has long been popular for use with both artificial and natural light. The Chinese favour brightly coloured, hand-painted paper lanterns to shade candles both in the home and the garden. Japanese lampshades, for both candles and electric bulbs, echo the style of shoji screens, with translucent paper stretched between square wooden frames.

In the West, paper lampshades reached their peak of popularity in the 1970s, when practically every home boasted a spherical paper shade adorning the pendant light fitting in the middle of the living room. The round paper shade is now regarded more as a cheap solution than a fashion statement, but paper shades are not completely *passé*. Ikea has recently introduced a floor-standing paper shade, a 1-m (3-ft) high white tube supported on a wire frame, which makes a modern statement in the corner of the room.

Treated paper can also be used for window blinds, either hung on their own or in addition to curtains. Paper blinds are not best suited for use in damp environments such as the bathroom or kitchen, where steam will damage them. However, the natural translucency of paper makes the blinds ideal as a light filter in a sunny living room or garden room. When pulled, the blinds remove the glare of the midday sun while retaining a degree of natural light. Blinds can easily be painted to make them more decorative or left plain white; if natural, unbleached paper is used the effect is softer and warmer. The blinds can be flat (for roller blinds), or folded into a neat concertina shape. Because paper works so well with light, and because it is affordable and easily replaced, it remains a favourite in the translucent portfolio.

mesh and grids

"You can put mesh furniture into open space and it retains the spaciousness."   James Gott,

furniture designer Although metal and wood are solid materials, they take on a transparent quality

when used in a grid structure. Metal mesh is the ideal material for the industrial interior, while

latticed wood screens conjure up romantic images of the harem, Ali Baba, and the Arabian Nights.

left Metal can be transparent. Wire furniture is sturdy and will provide
comfortable support, but it will not dominate in the transparent interior,
and the overall effect remains light and bright.

See-through materials such as glass, plastics, and sheer fabrics are obvious choices in the creation of a contemporary, transparent interior. But solid materials such as metal, wood, and concrete can also enhance an open-plan home when used as grids, grilles, or cast filigree-work. Depending on the gauge of the grid, the result can vary from barely visible to almost solid in response to the degree of openness or privacy required.

The Victorians were particularly intrigued by the use of metal as a decorative material. Once they had perfected the art of casting molten iron into surprisingly delicate designs, there was no stopping them. Not content with just creating decorative balustrades for balconies and stairways, they used cast iron in the manufacture of filigree benches, garden chairs — even ornate sewing-machine stands. The results of the Victorians' love affair with cast iron are still very much in evidence today, with heavy, decorative iron tables and chairs much sought after by antique dealers.

The paradox of strong, durable metal used in a lightweight, transparent way is a theme now adopted by contemporary designers, although the metal tends to be aluminium or steel rather than cast iron. Metal can be used for a wide range of furnishings, from barely visible wire mesh chairs to kitchen-cabinet doors that display their contents through a central panel of chicken wire. The use of metal for screens and room dividers is both practical and attractive. Screens made from wire mesh or sheets of steel punctuated with a punched-out pattern divide the room without blocking the light. They create an interesting, more substantial alternative to other transparent materials, while contributing to the industrial interior.

left Fine mesh can be incorporated into the transparent interior to provide gentle screening with a high degree of strength for areas such as stairs and raised walkways.

right These bathroom shutters incorporating ornate metal filigree provide privacy for those in the bathroom, while the lace-like effect of the metal work is thrown into sharp relief by the bright sunlight outside the window.

Today's metal designs tend to follow a more minimalist line than their ornate Victorian predecessors, but the juxtaposition of strength and transparency is no less intriguing.

The use of screens is on the increase, as loft dwellings and open-plan apartments become more and more popular. These large open living spaces can often lack intimacy, but the problem can be overcome by breaking the space down into designated areas, creating "rooms" within the larger environment. Another reason for the growth in demand for screens is the way we use our homes. Many of us no longer have the luxury of separate rooms allocated to a specific purpose, such as a designated dining room or spare bedroom. These rooms have become multipurpose, and might incorporate a home office, gym, or games area. By screening off a section of the room, you can keep one activity separate from another.

Metal may not seem the obvious choice of material for room dividers and screens, but it is a practical alternative, particularly for areas of heavy use or where a degree of strength is required. For instance, fencing off a balcony or stairway with a metal grille will allow visibility, while providing enough load-bearing strength to protect the user from falling.

Metal screens need not be utilitarian; there are designs available that can best be described as functional sculpture. Stephen Newby's design for UK company Full Blown Metals is created out of a series of inflated steel pillows. The pillows are joined to each other by their corners and then attached by rings to metal uprights so that sections of the screen can be folded back. Large spaces are left between the slightly crumpled pillows so that the screen does not completely block the view. The result is surprisingly soft in appearance and highly reflective, picking up images and colours from around the room as well as bouncing light back on to the floor and walls.

Andrew Tye has also been working in metal to create the Eileen screen for London company Tye 3D. In this multi-panelled aluminium screen, the panels pivot to create changing positive and negative spaces, and they seem to change colour depending on their angle.

left The clean, simple lines of this bar stool make it the perfect choice for a modern hi-tech setting. The stools would work equally well in a commercial bar or arranged round the counter of a domestic kitchen.

Designers of minimalist furniture have long favoured wire and steel rod as a material for realizing their designs. Charles and Ray Eames, the influential husband-and-wife American design team, created wire chairs back in 1952 which look as fresh and functional today as they did 50 years ago. Equally, Harry Bertoia's famous 1951 Diamond chair shows no sign of losing its popularity, as it still makes an appearance in the most contemporary locations. The simple, polished steel diamond-shaped seat provides comfortable support while melting subtly into the background.

Wire-mesh furniture is light yet strong. Its simple, angular shapes and uncluttered lines fit neatly into the modern interior while providing practical seating and storage solutions. Companies working in wire today include US company Knoll International, which has a range of wire furniture designed by Warren Platner, including a side chair with padded seat cushion and a coffee table with glass top. The base for the table and chair are made up of a multitude of rods that rise up and then fan out to support the tabletop or seat. Although these designs appear incredibly simple at first, they contain a great deal of eye-catching movement. The oddly named design label Moooi has been experimenting further with decorative techniques, and looks at ways to make steel furniture pretty. Its steel chair replaces the straight steel rods with a lace-like steel mesh incorporating a daisy motif. The chair is practical but looks less utilitarian than the other more geometric designs currently available.

Echoing the Victorian penchant for cast-iron garden furniture, contemporary wire-work chairs, tables, and planters are still popular for the conservatory or patio, either in natural or matt steel, or painted white. These romantic pieces add a certain elegance to outdoor dining without detracting from the delicate growth of surrounding plants.

Wire work can also be used for smaller items such as bread baskets and fruit bowls. These open-work vessels allow the contents to be readily visible so that their colours and textures becomes part of the whole. Metal furniture and accessories can fit into surprisingly varied settings: urban pavement café, city boardroom, industrial-style living room, or contemporary kitchen.

above Taking metal mesh furniture a stage farther, this seat design incorporates a curved back and shaped arms to emulate traditional upholstered furniture. The rest of the room remains partially visible beyond.

James Gott was inspired by café society to produce his contemporary range of steel furniture. When wandering around his home town of Manchester, he noted the massive growth in street cafés and the plethora of cheap-looking aluminium furniture positioned outside, which seemed to dominate the pavement. He studied 3D design at Manchester Metropolitan University, following a foundation course in art and sculpture, and started designing mesh furniture in 2000. "I found steel mesh to be a cheap material which you can bend and fold. It also lets the light through and you get gorgeous shadows." Shortly after he graduated, Gott's original designs were recognized for their practical simplicity, and he received the Allermuir Award for Furniture and the Blueprint Special Award for Creativity.

Gott's furniture is particularly suited to life on a Manchester pavement, as it not only provides comfortable, stackable seating but, in this particularly wet British city, it also allows rain to pass straight through so that the furniture can be in constant use.

The range, which is now produced under the Meshman label, started with a chair, table, and bar stool, and the aim has always been to create modern yet affordable pieces. A low chair and table and the upholstered Meshman sofa, a modular seating system, have since joined those first items. The company is also developing PVC pads for tables and chairs. Although originally designed for outside use, the Meshman range is equally at home in contemporary interiors where its clean simplicity contributes to a sense of urban chic.

The wire mesh for the furniture is produced flat and then bent into shape to create the different pieces. It can be supplied in its natural silver state or given a coloured epoxy coating in anything from white to vibrant orange. The chairs are sold for contract use in bars and cafés, as well as through a number of furniture retailers for use in domestic gardens and living rooms. The use of metal for outdoor furniture is certainly nothing new: the Victorians greatly favoured ornate cast-iron seating both for public and private gardens. James Gott's designs have taken this traditional theme and brought it bang up to date. The chairs are practical when exposed to the elements, while the use of mesh clearly positions them in the 21st century.

above Shown here in natural silver, this mesh can be given an epoxy coating in any colour. Chairs and tables can be made to match or deliberately contrast with their surroundings for an eye-catching statement.

right The concept is simple: stylish yet affordable furniture that is suited to use outside, even in wet climates. The wide gauge of the mesh means little water remains on the chair seat or tabletop, even after a downpour.

Micro-fine metal threads can be used in conjunction with synthetics, such as polyester, to produce shimmering metallic cloth. Surprisingly, copper, steel, bronze, and brass can also be used to create 100 per cent metal fabric.

Admittedly, this is not the most tactile of fabric and it does not drape gracefully into soft swags and folds. But metal fabric is dramatic, translucent, and strong. Wire cloth is woven in the same way as conventional cloth, and is manufactured by weaving transverse or weft wires through longitudinal warp wires. The wires are crimped during this process, creating a firm connection so there is no fraying as with conventional cloth. By varying the arrangement of the wires, different sizes of opening or aperture can be obtained, either square or rectangular. Wire cloth has a great many qualities that make it ideal for architectural and interior use. It has high tensile strength, high resistance to abrasion, good formability, smooth surface structure, and it is completely fireproof. This speciality cloth, which is available in a wide range of weights, materials, and designs, is suitable for use in room dividers, screens and large-scale curtains – such as safety curtains in theatres.

Janet Stoyel has been working with wire cloth for her company The Cloth Clinic in southern England, and has patented an innovative method for creating patinated effects. Precision woven-wire cloths are patterned by a process involving ultrasound scanners and lasers. The cloth retains its bright metallic appearance and natural characteristics but the colour of selected areas completely changes. These colours are governed by the metal's molecular content, so that, for instance, copper cloth, which is usually a dark orange, develops a rainbow tint, and bronze cloth becomes tinged with green. The effects created are permanent and the patterns may be random or geometric, varying from delicate watermarks to spots. Different degrees of coloration are obtained depending on the amount of treatment the cloth undergoes.

As the cloth remains pure it is readily recyclable, and as the patination treatment does not create any emissions in terms of paints and dyes the product is relatively eco-friendly.

above When copper cloth is given the ultrasound treatment, the surface throws back a rainbow pattern similar to the effect of oil on water. Metal fabric is completely flame-retardant and is therefore ideal for commercial use.

right A bed is screened from the rest of the room by a series of panels of metal fabric suspended from the ceiling. The panels are translucent and, unlike conventional fabric, keep their shape rather than moving in the breeze.

In many countries slatted wooden shutters serve a very useful purpose, as they keep out the glare of the midday sun yet still allow sufficient light to filter into the room. From quaint Mediterranean village houses to imposing colonial residences, wooden shutters create a mood of cool tranquillity, perfect for the afternoon siesta.

In the contemporary interior, adjustable slatted shutters can be used to make a feature of a window while providing a variable degree of privacy. Ideal for the bathroom, the slats can be angled to allow natural light in while totally obscuring any view into the room from outside.

The concept of using wood for screens is particularly popular in Asia and the Middle East. Delicately carved, ornate filigree-work is used extensively as partitioning, screening, and in window apertures. The screens allow the maximum flow of air to pass through and cool the darkened rooms, while allowing a tantalizing glimpse of what lies beyond — perhaps a colourful bazaar, marble courtyard, or private garden. Internally, carved wooden screens replace walls for the practical purpose of reducing the heat, although they also lend an air of romance to the room.

Wooden trellis panels have always been popular in garden design. They become part of their natural surroundings, as the screens allow plants to climb up, while also inviting exploration to what lies beyond. Contemporary wooden screens in the home serve much the same purpose: the solid sections of the work contribute aesthetically to the overall decorative theme, while giving just enough visible access to other areas of the room. Wood is an extremely pleasing medium, sitting comfortably with other architectural materials such as glass, stone, plastics, and metal.

Breaking away from the traditional design of lattice-work screens, the Italian design workshop Erica Inartemvertere has produced some innovative wood-based screens using flat, veneered panels hung loosely together. Each panel has a different pattern, and when combined they create an overall patchwork effect. The screens would look equally good hung against a white wall as a piece of artwork as they do suspended in a room to create a highly decorative internal wall.

above Slatted wooden blinds cover a full-height bathroom window. They are fully adjustable to allow as much or as little light into the room as required. When the sun is bright, shadow patterns are thrown across the wall and bath.

left Overhead lights have been completely dispensed with in this subterranean bar. Instead, the illuminated walls have been clad with irregular wood panels that create a highly effective textural surface.

Wood has an age-old pedigree as a material for furniture. Primitive man probably sat on roughly hewn logs, while every furniture designer since, from Chippendale to Conran, has made their name with wood.

It is perhaps this legacy that has led contemporary designers to look for ever more interesting ways to use this natural material, moving away from traditional carving and veneering to bending and shaping. The new generation of wood furniture is lightweight, fluid, and, most importantly, transparent.

Although solid like metal, wood can be used to create attractive pieces of furniture with an open structure that allows light to pass through and creates a different view of the piece from every angle. Designer Jane Dillon pushed the flexibility of wood to the limit when she created the gloriously undulating Mobius bench for the Science Museum in London, as part of its Challenge of Materials gallery.

Dillon used a timber-compressing technique developed in Denmark that makes solid wood extremely pliable. The resulting bench bears little resemblance to its garden-centre cousins, featuring beech slats worked into elegant curves and waves.

The wood used for Mobius is exposed to steam, which softens the cell walls sufficiently to allow the plank to be compressed along its length by up to 600mm (24in). This compression permanently shortens the piece and, in effect, concertinas the cell walls at a microscopic level, allowing them to fold and unfold rather like an accordion. The resulting wood can be bent and twisted in three dimensions, even when cold.

Australian Marc Newson is another contemporary designer taking a fresh look at wood. Newson is best known for his futuristic but technically rigorous approach to design, and has worked for studios in Tokyo, Paris, and London creating pieces in aluminium and plastic. His Wood chair, created in 1988 for the Italian company Cappellini, is made up of dozens of fine slats that curl round and back through themselves to create the seat. The chair has a delightful simplicity and yet is technically brilliant, as the fine slats are held in such a tight curl that there is no danger of splitting or splintering.

right A loose basket-weave structure has been used to create these sculptural wall lights. The cone-shaped shades throw light up the wall, while the open nature of the weave allows shards of light to produce a decorative pattern between the fittings.

left Jane Dillon's Mobius bench was designed to show just how flexible wood can be. A continuous loop of wooden slats undulates gently across the seat and back, culminating in generous arms.

"Glass has been promoted as the material of the future for the past five years. In fact it will probably continue to break new ground for the next fifteen." Stewart Hearn, First Glass

Transparent and translucent materials have captured the imagination, and as new technology continues to develop exciting possibilities for glass, plastic, fabrics, and mesh, the creative opportunities are far from exhausted.

left The biggest concern when working with glass is that it will break. George Papadopoulos has recognized this fear and exploited it, deliberately smashing large sheets of glass to create his anarchic designs.

left Used to house a space rocket, this building was created for NASA using ETFE.

right Design company Elecktrickery recycles waste plastic to create light fittings. This table lamp with its fine map of lines and dots is made out of four old circuit boards fastened together to make a box shape.

right The increased use of plastic in the production of everyday items is causing long-term problems in waste management. Fortunately, there are companies such as Elecktrickery who give our rubbish a new lease of life.

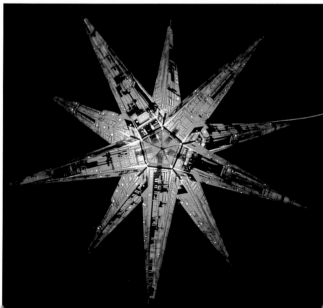

The enthusiasm for using transparent materials in domestic and commercial locations shows no sign of abating. Far from being a passing trend, widely visible, open-plan environments are becoming accepted into the mainstream, as people realize the benefits of living and working in bright spaces with maximum access to natural light.

Glass has led this interior revolution, with its increased use in architectural structures from walls to stairs and floors to ceilings. The strength and load-bearing ability of glass has been thoroughly explored and enhanced to make this material a viable alternative to traditional bricks and mortar.

World-renowned architects Foster and Partners have done much to encourage the acceptance of glass buildings in our urban landscapes. The partnership's visions for the German Reichstag refurbishment and London City Hall have not only resulted in impressive corporate buildings but also have created a greater sense of open dialogue between politicians and the public.

Now the partnership, headed by Sir Norman Foster, is in the process of creating its most awe-inspiring and futuristic building to date. Situated on the site of the former Baltic Exchange in the City of London, the 40-storey cigar-shaped office block will be the new HQ for Swiss Re. Already dubbed the "Gherkin", the 180-m (590-ft) tower is due to be completed in 2004. This radical development is made possible by the use of advanced computer design technology, developed in the aerospace and automotive industries for the creation of complex curved forms. Key to the appeal of the Gherkin is the fact that it is fully glazed, allowing occupants increased external awareness and the benefits of daylight in the work environment. The walls are constructed from two layers of glass, with a cavity that is ventilated with air drawn out of the offices. This enables solar radiation to be intercepted before reaching the interior, therefore reducing the building's reliance on air conditioning.

The increased use of glass in architecture has naturally lead to the exploration of other transparent materials, resulting in acrylic and

above The domes at the Eden Project look like giant, multi-faceted soap bubbles. They let in a maximum of light, and all the rain collected in the curved structures is used to water the plants.

right ETFE weighs less than one per cent of the equivalent-sized pane of glass, needs less steel to hold it up, and lets more light through. It is also recyclable and long lasting, with a life span of over 25 years.

polycarbonate sheet regularly contributing to the transparent interior. Plastic has long been regarded as the cheap alternative to more desirable products, but as designers find new and exciting ways to use it, playing to its unique qualities rather than using it purely as an economical alternative to glass, the true flexibility of this man-made material will emerge.

A fine example of this is the Eden Project — two huge conservatories set in an old clay quarry in Cornwall in southwest England. These conservatories, or Biomes, have been designed to create two completely different environments, the humid tropics and a warm temperate climate. In order for non-native plants from Mediterranean herbs to banana palms to thrive in Eden, they had to be warm and have access to plenty of natural light. Triple-glazed Ethyl tetra fluoro ethylene (ETFE) provided the answer. This lightweight material enabled the architects to design the conservatories as a series of geodesic domes. Glass was too heavy, too inflexible, and too dangerous for the project. ETFE is described by Eden as "clingfilm with attitude". It is a strong, lightweight, anti-static film that is highly transparent to UV light but is not degraded by sunlight. It is recyclable and has better insulation properties than glass. ETFE weighs less than one per cent of the equivalent-sized pane of glass, needs less steel to hold it up, and lets more light through. It is long-lasting, with a life span of 25 years, and tough — a single inflated pillow made of ETFE can take the weight of an entire rugby team. ETFE is also non-stick, so it is self-cleaning.

To make the transparent covering for the steel-framed Biomes, three layers of ETFE were heat-welded together at the edges and inflated into giant 2-m (6½-ft) deep pillows. The transparent pillows act like a blanket, letting in light and insulating the Biomes. The weightlessness of ETFE was perfectly suited to the design of the Eden Project Biomes, the largest of which measures 250m (820ft) long, 55m (180ft) high and 110m (360ft) wide (large enough to house the Tower of London) and has no internal support. Now that ETFE has proved itself at Eden, and in the construction of the beehive-shaped rocket housing at NASA in the USA, it is only a matter of time before we see the material in much wider use.

Plastic will also continue to break new ground in terms of furniture and furnishings. Ennemlaghi's revolutionary Cube Chair uses vibrant red PVC because it is the most suitable material for the design, not because it is a cheap alternative to leather or fabric. As plastics lose their utilitarian image designers will continue to push this diverse family of materials to the limit.

One of the key issues for the 21st century will be the better and more careful use of our resources. The transparent interior will play its part, allowing for a reduction in the use of artificial light and heat. However, as plastics are not biodegradable, their increased use is not always welcomed. The use of recycled materials will become increasingly important and designers are already looking at ways to re-use discarded plastic objects. Elecktrickery, for instance, is a young design company specializing in turning everyday rubbish into contemporary lights, with amazing results. One of their specialities is the use of printed circuit boards for table and pendant lampshades.

As well as designers finding ever more innovative ways to use plastics, there are those keen to introduce alternative materials into the translucent portfolio. Every year an enthusiastic new group of designers present their creations at degree shows worldwide. In recent years these shows have launched Janet Stoyel, with her fine-weave metal fabrics; the UK-based Diffuse team, Lucy Bilcock and Jason Boatswain, who create soft ambient light fittings out of porcelain; and Ned Atkinson who has invented wall-hung radiator panels clad in fibreglass. As transparent design continues to be popular there will be a greater use of diverse materials that add a degree of substance to a glazed interior, such as bendy wood benches and wire-mesh chairs.

But the material that started the transparent revolution should not be forgotten. The way glass is used will continue to evolve: designer George Papadopoulos, of London company Yorgos, has embraced a fundamental fear – that glass breaks – and incorporated sheets of shattered glass into his architectural designs. The transparent interior of the future will not be stark and featureless: screen-printed Perspex, jewel-bright UV resins, and chunky, textural-fused glass panels will bring rooms to life. Transparent materials will be more decorative, while still promoting the highest possible flow of light.

above The Elsie Chaise Longue, designed by Benson Saw and Voon Wong, is created from woven electroluminescent wire that is normally used in signage.

left A vision of the future? The cult 1968 sci-fi adventure *Barbarella*, in its depiction of the 41st century, included a scene where the beautiful young astronaut, played by Jane Fonda, was trapped inside a transparent prison.

Agape: Via Po Barna 69, 46031 Correggio Micheli di Bagnolo, San Vito, Italy
+39 0376 250311   www.agapedesign.it   PVC and acrylic bathroom fittings

Alessi: Via Privata Alessi 6, 28882 Crusinallo, Omegna, Italy
+39 0323 868611   www.alessi.it   Resin accessories

Andrew Moor Associates: 14 Chamberlain Street, London NW1 8XB, UK
+44 (0)20 7586 8181   www.andrewmoor.co.uk   Glass design consultancy

Bathrooms International: 54 The Burroughs, London NW4 4AN, UK
+44 (0)20 8202 8288   www.bathroomsint.com   Coloured glass basins

black + blum: 2.07 Oxo Tower Wharf, Bargehouse Street, London SE1 9PH, UK
+44 (0)20 7633 0022   www.black-blum.com   Designers of polypropylene lights

BoBo Designs: 10 Southampton Street, Brighton, Sussex BN2 2UT, UK
+44 (0)1273 684753   Acrylic lights and furntiue

Brunschwig & Fils: One Design Center Place, Boston MA 02210-2398, USA
+1 617 348 2855   www.brunschwig.com   Textile designers

B Sweden: Herrakra, S-360 73, Lenhovda, Sweden
+46 0474 23040   www.bsweden.com   Manufacturers of translucent glass lights

Cattelan Italia: Carre, Vicenza, Italy
+39 0445 318711   www.cattelanitalia.com   Translucent glass furniture

The Cloth Clinic: The Old Rectory, Sheldon, Honiton, Devon EX14 4QU, UK
+44 (0)1404 841350   Sheer metal cloth

Création Baumann: Weberei und Farberei AG, 4901 Langenthal, Switzerland
+41 062 919 6262   www.creationbaumann.com   Designer textiles

Curvet USA: 11999 Route 6, Corry, PA 116407, USA
+1 814 663 0704   www.curvetusa.com   Translucent and coloured glass furniture

Daedalian Glass: The Old Smithy, Cold Row, Carr Lane, Stalmine, Poulton-le-Fylde,
Lancashire FY6 9DW, UK   +44 (0)1253 702531
www.daedalian-glass.co.uk   Designer/producer of frosted and coloured glass artwork

Danielle Roberts: 12 Ruskin Court, Winchmore Hill Road, London N21 1QJ, UK
07813 787 176   Screen-printed acrylic furniture

David Colwell & Trannon: Chilhampton Farm, Wilton, Salisbury, Wiltshire
SP2 0AB, UK   +44 (0)1722 744577   www.trannon.com   Clear acrylic furniture

Dewhurst Macfarlane: 41 North Road, London N1 9ER, UK
+44 (0)20 7609 9541   Architects specializing in glass

Diffuse: 1 Jubilee Lane, Langford, Biggleswade, Bedfordshire SG18 9PH, UK
+44 (0)1462 638331   Manufacturers of porcelain lights

Edra: PO Box 28, Perignano (PI), Italy
+39 (0)58761 6660   www.edra.com   Designer PVC furniture

Electrickery: Unit 3K1, Cooper House, 2 Michael Road, London SW6 2ER, UK
+44 (0)20 7610 9877   Manufacturers of light fittings from recycled plastic

Ennemlaghi: 10 Palmerston Road, Londn N22 8RG, UK
+44 (0)20 7987 3946   Designer PVC furniture

FA Firman: 19 Bates Road, Harold Wood, Romford, Essex RM3 0JH, UK
+44 (0)1708 374534   www.firmanglass.com   Specialist glass installers, incl. stairs

Fiam Italia: Via Ancona 1/b, 61010 Tavillia, Italy
+39 0721 20051   www.fiamitalia.it   Designer textured-glass furniture

First Glass: Unit 2A, Union Court, Union Road, London SW4 6JP, UK
+44 (0)20 7622 3322   Coloured glass ornaments and lights

Forster Inc: 63 Redchurch Street, London E2 7DJ, UK
+44 (0)20 7613 5183   www.forsterinc.co.uk   Interior design practice

Foster and Partners: 22 Hester Road, London SW11 4AN, UK   +44 (0)20 7738 0455
www.fosterandpartners.com   Architectural practice specializing in large glass structures

Full Blown Metals: 12 Clarence Street, Ulverston, Cumbria LA12 7JJ, UK
+44 (0)709 212 6874   www.fullblownmetals.com   Manufacturer of designer
metal screens

Fusion Glass Designs: 365 Clapham Road, London SW9 9BT, UK
+44 (0)20 7738 5888   www.fusionglass.co.uk   Decorative glass panels

Glass Design: 51-63 Sangley Road, London SE6 2DT, UK   +44 (0)20 8698 7979
www.glass-design.net   Specialist manufacturer of UV bonded glass panels and furniture

Igloo: Porthmadog, Gwunedd LL49 9UG, UK
+44 (0)1766 512652   www.igloo.uk.com   Clear and textured glass bathroom fittings

Jane Dillon: Studio Dillon, 28 Canning Cross, London SE5 8BH, UK
+44 (0)207 274 3430   Designer of bentwood furniture

Jo Downs: 11 Merchants Quay, Penygillam Industrial Estate, Launceston, Cornwall
PL15 7ED, UK   +44 (0)1509 558320   www.jodowns.com   Designer of fused-glass panels

Jona Hoad: 178a Glyn Road, London E5 0JE, UK
+44 (0)20 8510 9828   Lighting designer working with acrylic

Kartell: Via Delle Industrie1, 20082 Niviglio MI, Italy
+39 02 900121   www.kartell.it   Manufacturer of furniture in a variety of plastics

Kate Maestri: 2.11 Oxo Tower, Bargehouse Street, London SE1 9PH, UK
+44 (0)20 7620 0330   Coloured-glass artist

Katy Holford: 8 Luton Road, Toddington, Bedfordshire LU5 6DF, UK
+44 (0)1525 872308   www.katyholford.co.uk   Designer of clear glass furniture

Kazuhiro Yamanaka: Unit 15, 109 Bartholomew Road, London NW5 2BJ, UK
+44 (0)20 8452 3018   Designer of illuminated polypropylene chairs

Kinnasand: Tullhus 3, Skeppsbrokajen, SE-111 30 Stockholm, Sweden
+46 0844 04400   www.kinnasand.se   Textile manufacturer

Knoll: 1235 Water Street, East Greenville, PA 18041, USA
+1 215 679 7991   www.knoll.com   Producer of resin panels

Lampholder 2000: Unit 8 Express Park, Garrard Way, Telford Way Industrial Estate, Kettering NN16 8TD, UK   +44 (0)1536 520101   www.lampholder2000.co.uk Polycarbonate light fittings

Mathmos: 20-24 Old Street, London EC1V 9AP, UK
+44 (0)20 7549 2724   www.mathmos.co.uk   Silicone lights

McKinney & Co: The Coach House Studio, 39 Urlwin Street, London SE5 0NF, UK
+44 (0)20 7627 5077   Decorative glass finials

Meshman: Level 1, 70 Tib Street, Manchester M4 1LG, UK
+44 (0)161 834 5085   Metal mesh furniture

Mono Tabletop: 2787 Margaret Mitchell Drive, NW Atlanta, GA 30327, USA
+1 404 352 1201   www.mono.com   Acrylic tableware

Moooi: 25 Weybrook Drive, Burpham, Guildford GU4 7FB, UK
+44 (0)1483 877875   Metal mesh furniture

Moss: 146 Greene Street, New York, NY 10012, USA
+1 212 226 2190   www.mossonline.com   Acrylic accessories

Ozone: Unit 1, Home Farm Business Centre, Home Farm Road, Brighton, Sussex BN1 9HU, UK   +44 (0)20 7351 0066   www.ozoneglass.co.uk Decorative glass panels

Propaganda: 779/210 Pracharajbumphen Road, Samsennoak Huay Kwang, Bangkok 10320, Thailand   +662 691 6331   www.propagandaonline.com Polypropylene lights and furniture

Raffoul Darrer Architects: Kings Yard, Annismore Avenue, London W4 1SE, UK
+44 (0)20 8994 2800   www.rdarchitects.com   Architects experienced in glass interiors

Ronald Schmitt Tische GMBH: Gretengrund 3 D, 69412 Eberbach/Neckar, Germany
+49 (0)6271 9490   www.ronald-schmitt.de   Clear glass furniture

Ruth Spaak: 91 Evesham Road, Stratford-upon-Avon, Warwickshire CV37 9BE, UK
+44 (0)1789 415244   Designer of woven glass screens

Sahco Hesslein: Kneuzburger Str 17, D-90471 Nuremberg, Germany
+ 49 0911 99870   www.sahco-hesslein.com   Textile producer

Skopos: Providence Mills, Earlsheaton, Dewsbury, West Yorkshire WF12 8HT, UK
+44 (0)1924 465191   www.skopos.co.uk   Specialist in textiles for the contract market

Smile Plastics: Mansion House, Ford, Shrewsbury SY5 9LT, UK
+44 (0)1743 850 267   Recycled plastic sheet

Stella Corrall: 13 Maitland Avenue, Chorlton, Manchester M21 7ND, UK
0777 6384550   Designer of PVC accessories and screens

Sottini: National Avenue, Kingston upon Hull HU5 4HS, UK
+44 (0)1482 449513   www.sottini.co.uk   Acrylic bathroom suites

Studio Warwick: 42 Burnaby Street, London SW10 0PL, UK
+44 (0)207 3523653   www.warwick.co.uk   Fabric supplier

Sturm und Plastic: Via Coti Zelati 90, Palazzolo Milanese, 20030 Milan, Italy
+39 02 9904 4222   Clear acrylic furniture

The Natural Tile Company: 150 Church Road, Redfield ,Bristol BS5 9HN, UK
+44 (0)117 941 3707   www.naturaltile.co.uk   Glass and resin tiles

Tom Schneider Designs: Unit 22, Station Close, Potters Bar, Hertfordshire EN6 1TL, UK
+44 (0)1707 644964   www.tomschneiderdesigns.co.uk   Designer of glass-topped tables

Totem Design: 2 Alexander Street, London W2 5NT, UK
+44 (0)20 7243 0692   www.totem-uk.com   Illuminated polypropylene furniture

Trevira: Lyoner Strasse 38a, D-60528 Frankfurt, Germany
+49 693 055756   www.trevira.de   Manufacturer of polyester thread

Tye 3D: Unit 8, Block A, 1 Fawe Street, London E14 6PD, UK
+44 (0)20 7536 9291   www.tye3d.com   Designer of metal screens

Yorgos: 31 Tower Gardens, London N17 7PS, UK
+44 (0)20 8885 2029   www.yorgosglass.com   Decorative textured glass panels

acknowledgments

The publishers would like to acknowledge and thank the following people,
who have kindly provided photographs for use in this book:

Front cover: Ray Main/Mainstream/C2 Architects
Back cover: Jon Bouchier/Red Cover

1 RHA Furniture; 2 Cini Boeri and Tomu Katayanagi for Fiam Italia; 5 Ray Main/ Mainstream; 6 Schoner Wohnen/Camera Press; 9 Ray Main/Mainstream; 10 Ken Copsey/Now/IPC Syndication; 13 Ray Main/Mainstream; 14 Andreas von Einsiedel; 17 Dennis Gilbert/VIEW/architect: Alsop, Lyall & Stormer; 18 Andrew Twort/ Red Cover; 20 Chris Gascoigne/VIEW/architect: Fletcher Priest; 21 Ray Main/ Mainstream/John Minshaw Designs; 22 Heidi Grassley/Axiom; 23 Winfried Heinze/ Red Cover/interior designer: Annie Stevens; 24 Defy Interiors; 25 Rolf Benz; 27 Narratives/Jan Baldwin/architect: Pierre Lombart; 28-29 Dewhurst Macfarlane and Partners; 30 Dennis Gilbert/VIEW/architect: Walter & Cohen; 32 Heidi Grassley/ Axiom/Seth Stein Architects; 33 Jake Fitzjones/Red Cover/Fulham Kitchens; 34-35 Verne; 36 Andreas von Einsiedel; 37 Tim Street-Porter/Elizabeth Whiting; 38 Geoffrey Drayton/EmmeBi; 39 Verne; 40 Andreas von Einsiedel/Red Cover/ designer: Tara Bernerd; 41 Foscarini; 44-45 Raffoul Darrer Architects; 46 James Mitchell/Red Cover/designer: Lulu Guinness; 48 Schoner Wohnen/Camera Press; 49 Cesar Color; 50-51 Andrew Moor/Graham Jones; 52-53 Andrew Moor/Kirsty Brooks; 54 Fired Earth; 55 Glamorous Co Ltd/Nacasa & Partners Inc; 56 Jado; 57 Nick Carter/Red Cover; 58 juicy glass; 59-61 Kate Maestri/Philip Vile; 62 Jon Bouchier/Red Cover; 64 Rodney Hyett/Elizabeth Whiting; 65 Ozone Glass; 66 Jo Downs; 67 Kim Sayer/Red Cover; 68-69 Ozone Glass; 71 Chris Gascoigne/ VIEW/Architect: Fletcher Priest; 72 James Mitchell/Red Cover; 73 Alan Weintraub/ arcaid.co.uk; 74 Fired Earth; 75 Chris Gascoigne/VIEW/architect: Pardy Yee; 76-77 Sturm und Plastic; 78 Graham Atkins-Hughes/Red Cover; 79 Ray Main/ Mainstream/designer: Jan Milne; 80 Tom Leighton/ Elizabeth Whiting; 81 above Guglielmo Galvin/Red Cove, below Verne; 82-83 Forster inc/photo: Tom Scott; 84 Trannon Furniture; 85 Ken Hayden/Red Cover; 86-87 Sturm und Plastic; 88 Bobo Design Ltd; 89 Lampholder 2000/designer: Neil Wilson/photo: Neil Wilson; 90 Sottini; 91 Alternative Plans/Agape; 92 Ray Main/Mainstream; 93 above Narratives/ Jan Baldwin, below Ray Main/Mainstream; 94 Sebastian Hedgecoe; 95 Dennis Gilbert/VIEW/Blauel Architects; 96 Ray Main/Mainstream/architect: Neil Fletchers; 97 Chris Dawes/Living etc/IPC Syndication; 98 Graham Atkins-Hughes/Red Cover; 99 Ray Main/Mainstream; 100 Edra; 102 Stella Corrall; 103 Craig Knowles/Living etc/IPC Syndication; 104 Narratives/Polly Wreford; 106 Kazuhiro Yamanaka; 107 Totem Design; 108 Mathmos; 109 Abbi Kiki; 110-111 Comma; 112-113 Burkett Design Inc; 114 Osborne & Little/Zari and Silvani Liberty Furnishings; 116 Creation Baumann; 117 Guglielmo Galvin/Red Cover; 118 Mulberry; 119 Brigitte/Camera Press; 120 Richard Powers @ redback.arcaid.co.uk; 121 Ken Hayden/Red Cover/Montevetro/designer: Jonathan Reed, architect: Lord Richard Rogers; 122 Skopos Design Ltd; 124 Kinnasand; 126-127 Création Baumann; 128 Andreas von Einsiedel; 129 Ken Hayden/Red Cover/designer: Jonathan Reed; 130 Brigitte/Camera Press;131 Fritz von Schulenburg/The Interior Archive/designer: Peter Hoffe/Serge Robin; 132 Schoner Wohnen/Camera Press; 133 Living at Home/Camera Press; 134 Henry Wilson/The Interior Archive/architect: Helen St Cyr; 136 Dennis Gilbert/VIEW/Blauel Architects; 137 Andreas von Einsiedel/Red Cover; 138 Ray Main/Mainstream; 139 Verne; 140-141 Meshman; 143 Artillery Architecture & Interior Design/Newbery Smith Photography; 144 Glamorous Co. Ltd/Nacasa & Partners Inc; 145 Rodney Hyett/Elizabeth Whiting; 146 Studio Dillon; 147 Ray Main/Mainstream; 148 Yorgos Ltd; 150 Nathan Willock/VIEW/architect: Nicholas Grimshaw & Partners; 151 Electrickery by firrm; 152-153 Peter Cook/VIEW/Nicholas Grimshaw & Partners; 154 Kobal Collection; 155 Elsie chaise longue, designer: Benson Saw, EL material: Surelight/photo: James Harris.